You Can Succeed With Your Preschool Class!

And TEACHING PRESCHOOLERS shows you how.
If you work with this important age group,
Dr. Ruth Beechick's TEACHING PRESCHOOLERS
will help you:

- Identify with the unique thought processes of the young child.
- Work within his basic learning and social abilities.
- Design effective handwork, song times, and visuals.
- Tell stories the children will listen to—and understand.
- Organize the classroom and the class time.
- Develop a sound personal philosophy of teaching.

TEACHING PRESCHOOLERS . . . a wealth of practical information and insight, written with care by a Christian specialist in children's education.

Teaching Preschoolers

Ruth Beechick

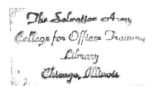

ACCENT BOOKS
Denver, Colorado

ACCENT BOOKS

A division of Accent Publications
12100 W. Sixth Avenue
P.O. Box 15337
Denver, Colorado 80215

Copyright © 1979 Accent Publications
Printed in the United States of America

Library of Congress Catalog Card Number 78-73252

ISBN 0-89636-019-9

Contents

Some folks plant the flowers
That bloom a day or two
Spreading cheerful fragrance
And every rainbow hue.

But I would plant a tree, Lord.
It will grow tall and strong,
And share its strength and shade
Long after I am gone.

PROLOGUE

In the Rocky Mountains where I live, I plant trees each year for reforestation purposes. Many of my trees are Ponderosa Pine. While these pines are not exactly Redwoods, or the Douglas Firs of my childhood, they are giants in their own right — straight, tall, long-needled evergreens. They impart a peace to those who love the trees. City people hike and picnic among them, sheltered from the heat and hurry of the life they know, finding renewal and strength for the days ahead.

I will see my seedlings grow from year to year, but I will never live to see the giants they will become. Yet I am compelled to plant them; the world needs them. And I am compelled to teach the children. I may be gone when they become giants — the spiritual giants the world so badly needs — but no matter; I teach them anyway.

The Lord has expanded this ministry to include teaching the teachers and developing curriculum for them to use. And that is how this book came to be. Everywhere I go I meet happy, super-busy preschool teachers struggling with one of the most difficult jobs in the church. This book is to help make their jobs easier and to train reinforcements for this ever-growing task.

Some of the teachers these days are men — brave souls, those men who tackle preschool classes. I apologize to them for referring in this book to the teacher as she. It probably doesn't quite compensate that I usually call the child he. Until someone invents a new kind of pronoun, our traditional way of writing is less awkward than saying that he or she did his or hers all by himself or herself.

This book is designed to be profitable reading for individuals who want to better understand preschool teaching. At the same time it is organized so it can be used in teacher training classes. The study helps in the appendix are for such groups, but individuals may want to try some of those too—particularly the observation tasks.

Though theory and practicality are mixed throughout, the first two chapters contain most of the theory. Readers who want to start with more immediately practical matters can begin reading with one of the later chapters, choosing whichever one will seem to help the most.

Ruth Beechick

1 What Are the Children Like?

Little children are fascinating to live with, to teach, and to study. We will be reviewing in these pages significant findings from the study of children, and considering some practical ways of helping them to learn, to help make our teaching job easier. But first we must define clearly just which children we are discussing.

What Shall We Call Them?

There is confusion about a name for the classes of young preschoolers. Most Sunday schools have a two-year program for those who are graduating from the toddler nursery and moving into the teaching program of the church. This class is variously called the nursery class, the preschool class, early childhood twos and threes, and other names.

These children usually aren't called *beginners,* because that name has traditionally been associated with a kindergarten age. *Early childhood* in its "official" use by government agencies and others in education refers to the full period from infancy through third grade, or about age 8, so this designation is not specific enough. *Nursery* is often used, but churches have a problem with people confusing it with the babies in the crib room or toddler room. Also, it tends to connote to parents that it offers baby-sitting rather than teaching. The term *nursery* is an old one and, with the recent proliferation of schools for the very young, the term *nursery school* came into use. Those who operated nursery schools, however, when they thought about it, realized that they were not nurses providing primarily physical care as the term implies, but they were teachers seeking to help in children's total development, with more and more emphasis on intellectual development as the public demanded it. Through them, the word *preschool* came into widespread use, and developed a new meaning. A child who attends preschool *is* a school child in his mind; his school is his preschool. This is the term we will use throughout this book.

How Old Are They?

Now, let us look at the ages included in the preschool class. Since the class is often referred to as the twos and threes, some churches move children into it immediately on their second birthdays. But experience has shown that a somewhat later age is more satisfactory. In state listings of licensed weekday preschools the large majority of schools are listed as taking children beginning at age 3, a few are listed as beginning at age 2½, and none at age 2. With the kind of program that preschools are offering, church preschools included, this slightly later age works better. At this time the best general recommendation for Sunday schools and similar church programs is to set 2½ as the starting age.

If some object and show concern about teaching those under 2½, then provide a "story lady" to come into the toddler room for a few minutes each Sunday. She can have a time of teaching through objects, pictures, books, songs and rhymes with any children who are ready for it. This will give the children a start in group learning but will not tax them with more structure than is suitable.

As the children turn 2½ they can be moved into the preschool class. There is no need to be rigid about this; some children may not be ready yet at this age, and can wait a bit longer to join the class. If the toddler room is close by, a new child might be allowed to go back to his familiar setting when he shows need for it. After a few Sundays of "trying out" the preschool class these children usually are ready to attend permanently. Some larger churches prefer to move children only in the fall, so that each fall all children who are 2 will begin preschool class. This makes the average starting age almost 2½.

Three-year-olds will be in, too, when the class begins each fall, and these children will be having birthdays all year long and turning 4. By the end of the year when it is time for promotion the following fall, the class of children who were 2 and 3 become a class largely composed of threes and fours.

This all may be so obvious that it seems superfluous to take space to write about it here, but in actuality it is a point of confusion in a great many churches. Teachers usually understand it; they see the birthdays happening week by week. But parents, Christian education committees, greeters, and others in the church do not have such a clear picture. The puzzle of the four-year-old looms particularly large. Parents become concerned that their own four-year-old is in a class of twos and threes and they want to move them on to the next class, not stopping to realize that those children are also having birthdays and are now becoming a class of fives and sixes. A door greeter spots a new family and, finding that their daughter is 4 he guides her to the kindergarten department without checking on the birthdate to see if perhaps this four-year-old belongs in the preschool class.

Church workers need to be made aware of these details of class arrangements, and parents need to be informed.

If people can learn to think in terms of school years rather than ages, it helps. Preschool children are 2 and 3 when the school year begins in the fall, and they are 3 and 4 by the time the next fall rolls around. It's as simple as that.

Larger churches will separate the two years of the preschool program, but otherwise the arrangements will be the same. Those who are 3 in the fall will be in their preschool class together until the following fall when they are moved on to the next department. By this time they are 4.

The Myths of Early Learning

What do we know about these children who are 2, 3, and 4? Is everything we read about them true?

In the last couple of decades we have seen what might be called the "age of the young child." We have seen enormous amounts of government money and other money go into promoting early childhood education. The promoters, much of the time, had their hearts — or other motivations — before their heads. With often good intentions, such as improving the lot of mankind and making everybody smarter than they were born to be, they poured massive resources into this effort. And now, looking back, some have the courage to admit it was one of the biggest efforts for the smallest returns that we have ever made.

To make the most of our own Christian education efforts in this area, we need a realistic view of what can be accomplished. We need to see some of the myths for what they are.

First, the myth that children do half their learning by the age of 5. It really is surprising that such a myth has grown up at the same time that we all believe the mind is not fully formed until the middle or late teens. How can we expect a partially formed intellect to learn more in a few years of inexperience than a fully developed mind can learn in mature years of study? But this is precisely what the myth advocates. There may be a large dose of wishful thinking here — a hope that we can solve our inadequacies in the next generation — perhaps even a Messianic hope that we can bring about a better world by developing the intellect of our young.

Often the myth can be traced directly to Benjamin Bloom's work where he concludes, in effect, that the mind is half-formed by age 5. But people have misused this research; they confuse development with learning. To say a mind is half developed is not to say it has learned half of what it will ever learn. Bloom's results, even when understood correctly, still present us with problems. To compare the mind of a three-year-old with that of a thirty-year-old is a little like comparing violets with rhododendrons. How many violets does it take to make one rhododendron? Statistics do not provide a way to answer this question. Bloom's statistics in this work are highly sophisticated, but he is limited by statistics itself; this system cannot adequately describe the complexity of the human mind. We can tell what color the flower is, or measure how high it is, or count how many petals it has, but any description of a flower is less than the flower itself. That is, it takes into account only some aspects of the flower. So it is with statistics and the human intellect.

A further problem with this kind of scientific work is the difficulty of defining just what intellect is. Various developers of mental tests have various definitions, and there is no consensus today of just what constitutes intelligence. So the problem is more difficult than comparing a violet and a rhododendron; it becomes a problem of comparing two unknown flowers.

This discussion of Bloom and statistics and the scientific study of the mind is not to deprecate such scientific studies; these studies are good and extremely useful to educators, psychologists and all of us. But what we are trying to do here is show how easy it is to fall into error by quoting a scientific study in another context. We need to be careful whether we are talking about petals, or color, or something else. In this case the disastrous error revolves around the use of the word *learning*. Bloom was not studying how much learning takes place, yet this is the misteaching that has followed his work.

Another possible source of this myth about the power of the child mind, is an earlier quote by Roman Catholics to the effect that if they have a child till the age of 7 they will have him for life. This quotation had no scientific basis at all but rested on everyday observation. Our own observation will tell us that there is much truth in this. We have always believed in raising our children by the Bible, bending the twig the way we want it to grow, and so forth. But when we make an educational "law" out of this we create problems. The negative side of the law would say that if we fail or miss in the early years all is lost. What a hopeless situation for many unfortunate children! The message of the gospel is precisely the opposite. God can make a person new and overcome the effects of misused early years.

In the area of intellect it is obvious that we can learn things now that we missed learning as children. Of course children can be damaged by gross neglect and by limited opportunity for normal development. But with children who have reasonably normal growing environments, we do not need to walk in fear that something we do or don't do will permanently mar their mental development. Neither should we have illusions that we can create a more intelligent individual by pushing things along just right.

This latter illusion is another myth that has grown up more recently than the one about the five-year-old. Being of recent vintage, the origin of this myth is easy to locate. In work with deprived children who have not developed normally, educators have been able to raise their tested mental levels. People have jumped onto these results and have promoted the false hope that we can also raise the mental levels of children who are developing normally. Here again is the Messianic hope that mankind can better himself by his own efforts—in this case, by educational efforts.

It is interesting that this work of helping deprived children to develop and make up for lost time nullifies the "all is lost" theory. It is true on one side that all is not lost if a child gets a later start than he should, and it is true on the other side that early teaching is not going to develop him beyond the normal.

The Myth of Attention Span

Various formulas are given to arrive at an attention span for children, given in terms of minutes. A common one is the child's age plus one. Thus, a child of 3 is said to have an attention span of four minutes. This is not only a myth, but it is an unhelpful way to think of attention. Instead of thinking of attention in terms of minutes, it is more helpful to think in terms of tasks. Is a task an appropriate level of difficulty for a child, and does the child stick with a task until it is finished? These are more helpful questions to ask. At the proper level of difficulty, a child can, and more often should, give his attention. But something that is beyond him should not claim his attention.

The myth of attention span lengths began with some early research on how long children gave attention to certain teacher-imposed tasks. These were measured in experimental conditions where the children were confronted with the tasks. If the researchers had observed little boys in natural conditions playing with their trucks, or had observed children pouring sand through various utensils, or a child sitting on Mother's lap looking at books, they would have obtained quite different results. All who work with children know that at times, in certain tasks, children's attention spans can be surprisingly long.

So there is nothing inherent within a child that limits his attention to a certain specified time; time is not the appropriate feature for us to study in this regard. Other studies will help us more. We should ask what kinds of things will attract children's attention, what qualities about the activities are important—difficulty level, kinesthetic (movement) features, visual features, and so forth. How shall we dress the things we want children to give attention to? How can we make our story time or teaching time as attractive as the trucks?

We need to learn not to talk in terms of attention span at all, but simply in terms of attention.

The Myth of Sharing

The myth of sharing is different from the preceding myths in that it does not have its origins in the misinterpretation of research. It seems to be peculiarly a Sunday school or Bible school myth. Bible teachers, anxious to teach children "Christian" behavior lessons, have latched on to the idea of sharing as an appropriate one to teach young children. Sometimes it may be that there are not enough crayons or blocks to go around and teachers hope to solve their problems by teaching sharing.

However that may be, the concept of sharing is not within the cognitive abilities of these young children. In one classroom three-year-old Jason was trying to pull a toy away from another child, all the while screaming, "He won't share. He won't share." In another classroom a teacher took a paste brush from two-year-old Tally and gave it to Jon to use for a moment. Tally had a meager vocabulary and knew no way to speak up in her own behalf, and the experience of being in a class group was new and bewildering anyway, so she simply remained sitting where she was and did nothing. The teacher said, "See how nicely Tally shares her brush with Jon."

To some children sharing means, "I have to give away my crayon." To others it means, "He should give me what I want." To others, like Tally, it has little meaning at all. Sharing involves seeing a shared viewpoint, and this is an advanced mental ability. Young children are learning to see the world from their own viewpoint, learning to separate themselves from their world, and learning to interract with their world. Later, when they have a better grasp of their own position and viewpoint, they can begin to understand another person's position and viewpoint. Then true sharing can be learned.

In the meantime, children can learn about taking turns. A child can learn that if he waits a little his turn will come again, but the wait had better not be too long. He also can learn to see the pleasure another child has in taking a turn. This will be a step on the way toward sharing. As for the crayons and paste brushes, the teacher can solve her problem by getting enough to go around. This is no more expensive than the "sharing" system. Eight boxes of crayons will last eight times as long as one box in the same class of eight children.

How Do Children Think?

The limitation of the child's viewpoint to his own is called egocentrism. This is not a disease; it is not selfishness, but a normal characteristic of the early years of life. In egocentrism, the child is the center of his world, he looks from his center outward, and that is the only view he has. Older people can to some extent imagine themselves in other positions and other situations and look from any one or more of those viewpoints as well as their own. But not so with young children.

The idea of egocentrism comes from Piaget's theory of mental development, and in more recent years Jerome Bruner and others are objecting that the child can in some ways see another's viewpoint, so this may possibly become a controversial issue at some time after this writing. But if it does, the Piaget idea is not likely to be proved "wrong"; it will only be refined and adjusted in some of its details.

The Character Research Project of Union College, which has been working for many years on this kind of problem, publishes results that agree with Piaget theory. In some of the "Bruner school" research, children are asked to give instructions to another person in order to see if they can take the other's viewpoint, and it is said that they do. More research is needed to determine what accounts for these results. Perhaps some of it comes from visual and external concrete cues, and not from inwardly projecting to another's viewpoint. Also, in matters of empathy—feeling along with others—there are aspects involved which are not purely logical, and Piagetian theory concerns the development of logical thinking. So even though some corners may be rounded off the present theory, the idea of egocentrism is an important one, and will be with us for a long time. Those who work with young children will do well to understand it.

For a concrete look at egocentrism, we can imagine a mountain experiment similar to one Piaget devised. You are on one side of some mountains and asked to draw what you see, so you draw the mountains like this.

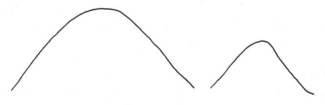

A big mountain and a little mountain—simple enough. Now you are asked to imagine you are on the other side and draw what you would see over there. If you are a mechanic or draftsman you don't hesitate, but otherwise you may think a moment and then come up with this.

A little mountain and a big mountain. You have projected yourself to another position and made a mental image of the opposite view. In your mind you imagined the other view, and you drew it. Your children cannot do that at all. They are a long way from performing like this on concrete objects, and even farther from performing so on abstract ideas.

Notice the similarity of the words image and imagination; they have the same root. Imagination is the ability to make mental images. A good imager can make images of things which do exist, which might exist, and even of something which does not exist but would be nice if he could invent it or write it or paint it or otherwise bring his image into existence.

Children are not good imagers. They do not have developed imaginations at all. A child may make a remark or draw a picture that causes an adult to say, "My, what an imagination that child has." But the child is simply responding to life in his limited egocentric way and imaging things from his one-way viewpoint. The adult should not read into the child's actions all the mental processes that may be involved in his own. Instead of commenting on the child's imagination, the adult should say, "I certainly would never have thought of looking at it that way. The child's view gives me a fresh view of this."

When a child roleplays—when he plays the part of a parent or teacher, for instance—he is showing some of the first signs of reaching out from his one viewpoint. This does not mean he has transcended egocentricity, but it is one of the ways he will try on and practice other roles, and with long practice and much experience he will eventually transcend his egocentricity. This is one of the values of roleplaying, and you can encourage it in the classroom.

Roleplaying can be called a symbolic function. It is an act that stands for the real thing, and thus is a symbol of the real thing. A child playing house acts in some ways like a mother, but she is not a mother. Play, then, is a symbol.

Pictures also are symbols, mental images are symbols and, most important of all, words are symbols. The ages from 2 to about 7 or 8 are known as the period of symbolic function. It contrasts with the first two years of life where images play little part. For the tiny infant the rattle exists only as long as he can see it, but hide it behind your back and it is gone; it simply does not exist for the infant, until the time he can form a mental image of it. Then he may reach and try to retrieve the rattle that exists for him even though out of sight. The infant under 2 similarly has little use of words and other symbols.

But the child over 2—those normal children in your preschool class—have entered the symbolic stage. They now can begin to extend their thought by means of symbols. This is where most of your teaching efforts should lie. You will provide wide experiences with symbols. You will introduce new symbols and continually expand the child's world. He needs new experiences and the symbols for those experiences. If something is soft and blue he needs not only to feel it and see it, but he needs the words *soft* and *blue* to help him extend the experience beyond the immediate sensory experience.

It is controversial whether the word comes first or the thought comes first. Some theories tend toward teaching that the thought comes first; it is rooted in the sensorimotor experience of feeling and seeing soft and blue, for instance. Other theories tend toward teaching that we need words or other symbols to think with. We would ignore the difference between blues and greens, for instance, unless we have to categorize them by sorting them or calling them different names. These differences are ignored in some cultures, just as Spanish-speaking people do not differentiate between *b* and *p* sounds, while English-speaking people do.

Whether the word or the thought comes first does not matter a great deal to teachers. We give wide, varied and repeated exposure to both experience and symbols. We let thought and word grow together. We use pictures, we allow symbolic play, we encourage talking. Symbols and the experiences which give meaning to them are the main thrust of our teaching in the intellectual sphere.

An important thing to know about the young child and his symbolic thought is that he does not perform mental operations with his symbols. We say, in Piagetian terms, that he is at the preoperational stage in his thinking. The child can have a mental image of the two mountains and he may have words for mountain and for big and little, perhaps even for left and right. All these symbols of thought he may have acquired, but one important function he still lacks. He has not yet interiorized these so that he can perform the mental operation of rotating the mountains (or himself) in his thought so that he can "see" them from the other side. Thus, we say he is in the preoperational stage of thinking.

Words are concrete to the child even though our meaning may extend farther. When a child climbs onto

Daddy's lap and says "Love me," his meaning may be closer to "Hug me" in adult language. But, of course, there is no sharp line between concrete and abstract, and many of the words we use with children are abstract, in spite of our efforts to the contrary. But there is no harm in this. Children have a long way to go to build the abstractions they will need later, and they have to start somewhere. It all starts in the concrete.

To summarize, the child's thought is:

(1) Egocentric, proceeding from his own self outward.

(2) Symbolic, extending his thought of actual experience by making use of symbols such as mental images and words.

(3) Concrete: his symbols stand for concrete things.

(4) Preoperational, since he does not yet manipulate his symbols in mental operations.

A preoperational child has limited concepts of time, space, relationships, and causality. These features of the child's thinking are described and illustrated in Chapter 5.

Social-Emotional Development

Children's feelings are usually very near the surface, and their actions are clues to you of their inner lives. They are in the early stages of learning to handle their feelings and act "socialized." Preschool experience should help the children in this process. Learning to know themselves and their feelings, learning to interact with others, learning to accept and feel good about themselves, feeling a security in their world—these are some of the many tasks of this stage of life.

These aspects of a child's development cannot be separated from his intellectual development; the child's personality is one integrated whole. Emotional growth is necessary to intellectual growth, and intellectual growth is necessary to learning to handle relationships with others. Everything is completely intertwined, and they are separated in books such as this simply for convenience in discussing and learning about the child.

Even though we cannot separate the various aspects of personality, it probably is correct to say that in these preschool years the child's teacher should give more attention to emotional growth than to the intellectual. Abraham Maslow's well-known hierarchy of needs will show this.

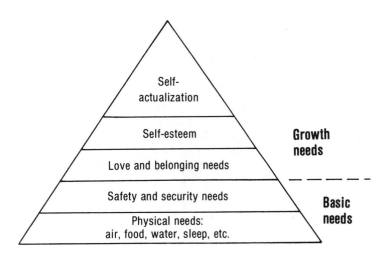

The first two steps on this pyramid are known as the basic needs. If they are not met, nothing higher can happen. But if parents, in the first two years of the child's life, provide him with his physical needs in combination with their caring, protecting presence, then the child finds his safety and security needs well met. When he feels secure in his home environment he can also come to feel secure in his classroom environment, and this basis is needed in order to reach any higher on the pyramid.

The security spoken of here is not only the physical security of a safe place where the child is not in danger of being hurt but, more importantly, it is a psychological security. He must be secure in his explorations and learnings and experimentations. He should not meet with rebuff and criticism for the things he does. If he fails—if parents and teachers think his efforts are not good enough—he will not have the security he needs to learn well.

When parents—and later, teachers—see that the child's basic needs are met in an atmosphere of love and acceptance, then the child's love and belonging needs are met and he can feel good about himself. These needs, you will notice, are higher on the pyramid than the basic needs. They are called growth needs—the needs of love and self-esteem. A child whose growth needs are being met is a child developing normally in many ways. He will be learning; you could hardly stop that, any more than you could stop his physical growth.

With this picture of the children's development before us, it is easy to see that the role of the preschool teacher is largely to help each child feel secure and feel good about himself. The room may be equipped with books, pictures, crayons and other items associated with academic learning, but all the learning activities should be seen as vehicles for the children to grow as persons.

Into every preschool classroom will come children with all kinds of problems in their development along these lines and there are no easy formulas for teachers to use in meeting these. The teacher should be well up the pyramid of emotional growth herself. If she feels insecure and inadequate and tries to help fulfill her own needs by pushing the children then she cannot help them. But a fulfilled teacher who knows God and loves the children will find many ways to help. Study of children, experience in working with them, and personal growth will continue to add to a teacher's effectiveness.

Spiritual Growth

Jesus said we must become as a little child if we would enter the kingdom of Heaven. Just how young a child He referred to, we do not know, but we do know that Jesus surely loves all the little children in our preschool classes and the children can be learning to love Him.

A child from a God-fearing home, who has his security needs met, is learning to trust. He first trusts parents, teachers and others in his world, and later, from this trust, he will learn what it means to trust God. A child who in his early years receives love and gives love to those in his immediate world will later know how to love God. A child who knows a loving father can see God as his loving heavenly Father. A child taught to obey parents and others in authority can later learn to obey God.

Love, trust, obedience—these are some of the foundations for spiritual growth. There are more—joy, awe, wonder, appreciation of beauty. Even learning to feel good about oneself is a step toward loving others as oneself. The deepest parts of a person, the whole person is important to God and to the body of Christ.

In one sense the spiritual life begins with the new birth, and one might argue that spiritual growth does not begin until the spirit has been made alive by the indwelling Holy Spirit. But there surely are things we can do to nurture the child along until that time. God made the human to be dependent longer and to develop more slowly than any other creature, and there no doubt are more advantages to this than we will ever know. There are more uses for this time than our research can uncover. But a human in relationship to another human knows things science does not know. A teacher nurturing a growing child depends not on formulas and techniques, but on a human relationship—and on God.

The spiritual growth of a child encompasses all other

kinds of growth. It is the child developing according to God's plan.

READING CHECK

1.   It is usually better not to enroll children in a preschool class before the age of 2½. T F

2.   Children, on the average, have accomplished half their learning by age 5. T F

3.   Children can have quite long attention spans under certain conditions. T F

4.   Sharing is one of the earliest behavior concepts that children can learn. T F

5.   Egocentrism refers to the natural selfishness of children. T F

6.   Preschool children are not yet good at using symbols to perform mental operations. T F

7.   Meeting a child's physical needs and love needs helps him develop an adequate self-concept. T F

8.   Spiritual growth is separate from other kinds of growth. T F

Answers: 1—T, 2—F, 3—T, 4—F, 5—F, 6—T, 7—T, 8—F

2 What Can Children Learn?

We can set more realistic goals if we know better what our children are like and what they are capable of learning. The previous chapter described characteristics of the preschool child, and this chapter will set out possibilities for his learning. The discussions in these two chapters are closely related, naturally, because we are simply thinking here about two sides of the same thing. In the one case we say the child is, for instance, egocentric and in the other case we say that the mountains the child images or draws are in such and such a position. That is, our words apply in one case to the child and in the other case to the mountains or other "content" of his learning. But the phenomenon that gives rise to our two descriptions is the same one.

In this chapter the emphasis of our discussion will be more on the content of children's learning. We will be trying to answer the questions of how many and what kind of mountains the child can learn about. The chapters on handwork, stories, music and games give additional information of this kind.

Bible Learning

Jesus and God. Researchers with a liberal theology have come to the conclusion that preschool children confuse Jesus and God, since they attribute the same

characteristics to both. That is, a child may say that Jesus made everything and God made everything, or that Jesus can do anything and God can do anything. Such "confusion" does not disturb those who believe that Jesus is God. The children's understanding in this is not incorrect, it is only incomplete. Later they will develop fuller understanding which encompasses earlier ideas but goes beyond them. Of course, our understanding of God will always be incomplete, even as adults.

The child's idea of this Jesus-God person can include these things: (1) He made things — flowers, rain, the child, everything; (2) He loves the child; (3) He is with the child; (4) He hears the child talk to Him; (5) He takes care of the child; and (6) He lives in Heaven. In addition, the child can sometimes think of Jesus the baby and God the Father. Or he can think of Jesus as a boy or man who did specific things in the stories he hears. While there are some things he will say about Jesus that he does not say about God, this does not mean he contrasts them and sees a difference; it simply happens as he thinks one thing at a time.

Seeming contradictions, such as that God is with us yet He lives in Heaven, are no problem at all. The child does not relate things, or does not have logic enough to see the apparent contradiction, so he is not puzzled about it.

Each of the ideas about God listed above is taken in a concrete way. For instance, for a child to say "God made everything" does not mean he thinks of God as Creator in the abstract sense that we do. The child can think that God made flowers or trees or any other specific item, and to say that God made everything is to make the same kind of concrete statement. It is a way of naming what God made.

It is similar with the phrase "God takes care of us." The idea of taking care is a rather abstract one, since it includes a large number and wide variety of specifics. A child can think concretely that God gives us food, that He helps us not to be scared in the dark and so forth. We use such concrete instances and teach children to name things that God does. So if we say God takes care of us, that is another name that children can learn to say. The meaning children attach to this is likely to depend on where else the word *care* is used in their lives. One child may think of taking care in his home as a baby-sitter does, for instance, if that has been his experience with the word care. Another child may not have a meaning to attach to it.

In teaching the children you need to continually use concrete examples to show what God made or what He can do or how He takes care of us. The word *love* is very abstract, too. Children learn love more in an emotional way than in an intellectual way. If a child is surrounded with love and he learns from loving people that Jesus loves him then the meaning sort of soaks into him. He feels it rather than cognizes it.

Teachers trying to help children understand Jesus have used various approaches. Some explain that Jesus is the God-Man. This perhaps succeeds in getting across the idea that there is something special about Jesus. No one else is called the God-Man—only Jesus. Some teach that Jesus is God's Son. This has the same effect; it is a special name used only for Jesus.

One or the other of these approaches seems necessary if we are to avoid giving the idea that Jesus is like other men. These are special names used only for Jesus. When a child uses these terms we should not assume that he understands the relationships inherent in them—the God and man combination relationship, or the Father and Son relationship. But neither should we declare that this is a misteaching because the children take these words concretely. Having these names and understanding them concretely is a first step toward fuller understanding later.

Prayer. To a preschool child prayer is whatever his experiences are with prayer. If his family has times of prayer at home, if his teacher and the children pray at Sunday school, then these acts of praying, to him, are what prayer is. A child can be taught to pray at other times and places. If Alex does something with Billy you can pray with Alex and say, "Thank You, God, for my friend Billy." This extends his idea of prayer by one more experience. A child can learn that he may pray when he is scared, or hurt, or glad.

From prayer experiences the child sees that prayer is talking to God. He can learn to thank God and to ask God for help. He could also learn to tell God he loves Him, or to tell God that He is good. Whatever a child can say to a parent, he can say to God; he tends to think of God in parental terms.

The Bible. The child's idea of the Bible comes just as his idea of prayer. That is, his experience with it determines his meaning. It *is* his meaning.

We have an easier time teaching what the Bible is than we do teaching about God or prayer, which are unseen. For teaching about the Bible we have a book, with pages, with words on them. The child can see the book, handle it, open it, say some of the words with you. We can give it special names — God's Book, the Book of God, God's Word. We can say the book has God's words in it. All these names are like our names for Jesus; they help to teach that this is a special book, but the abstract meaning we attach to a term like "God's Word" is not in the child's thinking.

Children can begin learning that they should love the Bible — again, by concrete means. "We love the Bible, so we close it carefully." "We love the Bible, so set it here where it won't fall." Just as you would show a child how to love his baby brother at home — hold him carefully, hand him a rattle, and so forth — so you show him how to love the Bible. The child needs help in knowing what to do. Show him how to turn pages, how to close the Bible (without slamming it), where to set it when he is through.

Getting out the Bible and "reading" some words each week—giving some attention to it in preschool class — is important if we would begin teaching what the Bible is. The reading may be only a few words, such as "[Jesus] is in heaven" (from John 3:13). Not only does handling and reading the Bible help in teaching one of our major Christian concepts, but it is good prereading experience for children. We know well how the children who have experiences with books do better in reading than those who do not have such experiences. So we who have the greatest Book of all do not need to stand by while children have their first book experiences, and then while they learn to read, and then — much later in life — bring them to our Book. We may as well begin at the beginning with the children. One four-year-old said, "I want to learn to read so I can read the Bible."

Good and Evil. We must realize that these are highly abstract ideas even though they seem simple to us, and it is not easy to teach them to children. The approach to use here is the same as with all abstractions—we begin with individual, specific instances. A child can learn that it is good to do this or bad to do that. He can learn that God wants him to do certain things. But admonitions to "be good" are not so understandable. The child needs to learn the word good, and learn that God likes him to be good—he may learn the Bible words "Do good"—but only the day by day incidents that are labeled good and bad will help him build meaning for these ideas.

A few children of preschool age come to the realization that they are not good, as God wants, and they need Jesus. But most children, being carefully taught, will be saved at a later age.

Bible Stories. In our day when there is so much study about what a child can learn and what he cannot learn, and so much concern about teaching Bible early anyway, there is a tendency for people to get uptight about which stories are chosen for use with children. On the one hand are people who think children should learn about the major Old Testament characters—in chronological order. And on the other hand are people who ask, "Why should they learn about Abraham?" They worry about the "life application" or about "meeting the needs" of the children. It seems the time is right now for us to laugh a little at ourselves and at our controversies over these matters. Actually many Bible stories can help meet a child's growth needs. The child may as well be growing with rhymes and pictures of Noah's ark, as of Mary's lamb or Jack's house. He may as well know of the strong man Samson as of Simple Simon. He can practice phonics with Josiah and Hilkiah as well as with Tommy Tittlemouse or Daffy-down-dilly. He may as well be neighing and baa-ing with Bible animals as with zoo or farm animals.

There is much in the Bible to use as growing material. There is much to help in children's learning of phonics, vocabulary, use of language, story sense, images of people and things. There is much to help build their concepts of God, Jesus and other important learnings. Bible stories have much to contribute toward the Christian education of preschool children.

Often overlooked, is the fact that stories can be repeated just as songs are. Children like to hear their stories over and over — in rhyme form, picture book form, flannelgraph form or whatever. By repetition they often learn the stories by heart and can tell them themselves. We should not limit this repetition learning to just songs and rhymes but should extend it to stories as well.

Cognitive Learning

Cognitive learning refers to the intellectual aspect of development. Preschool children are in what can be called the symbolic period of their mental development which extends from age 2 to about 7 or 8, as described in Chapter 1. Children's major mental work during this time is to acquire many symbols. Symbols are the materials the mind needs for thinking, and classroom teaching should provide opportunities and promote the learning of symbols. A discussion follows of three major kinds of symbols — words, pictures, and images.

Words. Probably the most significant development of a preschool child is his growth in the use of spoken language. From age 2 to 4 the average child's vocabulary increases from 150 words to 1500 words. This is a tenfold increase in the span of two years. Most of these new words are names of things. There are numerous ways that you can help children learn names of things in the classroom — names of real objects, pictured objects, and actions. Have the children say words after you. Encourage them to talk about things. Use conversation as one of the activities in your group teaching time. Use conversation during snack time and at every other opportunity. Learn to see children's talking as one of the most important things that happens in class.

Words that children use can be quite misleading to us if we are not skilled at understanding the child's mind. There can be a tendency to read into a child's talk much more than is there. If we project our meaning and our understanding behind the words he uses, we give him credit for being much more mature than he is.

After the advent of television there was a time when some declared that the TV generations of children were getting a head start in life — that they were learning more and learning it earlier and thus would go farther than previous generations found possible. Now time has dimmed that hope, and a closer look has revealed the superficial character of TV learning. Children may indeed talk of sea creatures of the South Seas rather than of what they might have learned in their own back yards if they had no TV. Their vocabularies may be sophisticated but their mental development remains at what is normal for children of their age.

So when we speak of learning words we are not holding out illusions that words *are* learning. On the other hand, we do not want to be afraid of teaching words. There is a view abroad that says we should not teach a Bible verse or a song without making sure the children first know the meaning. This is a rather extreme view, since it seems to separate meanings from words and assume that we somehow can feed in the meaning totally and then follow it by feeding in the word.

It is closer to the truth to realize that meanings and words grow together. First of all, a child does not learn a word upon one contact with it. He must hear it and use it a number of times before it becomes his. As he meets the word in specific instances and in varied contexts he builds up a better idea of its meaning.

Secondly, a child has various levels of vocabulary. Adults do too. There are some words you understand if you hear them in a speech or read them in a book, but they are not yet so much a part of your mental equipment that you use them yourself. Children experience the same kinds of levels. Many of the words you use have some meaning as children hear them in context. They may begin to use these words in mimicry without much meaning, and eventually the words settle down to the level where the children use them with more meaning.

Words are a legitimate part of our teaching. Bible words and other words important to Christian life are basic — words like obey, wise, love, good, bad; words like God, Jesus, Bible, Noah, Peter. We should be teaching them and letting children grow up with them. To do otherwise is to abandon our children to TV monsters, Coco-Cola, and Pooh Bear until they are older and can think better and can learn our words more quickly.

So what we need is a balance. We need to teach words — not in isolation, but in a rich learning environment, in varied contexts. And at the same time we should not fool ourselves about the maturity of the children's thinking when we hear them beginning to use the words we teach.

Pictures. Pictures are another major kind of symbol that we use as fuel for thought. They have become so ordinary to us that we have difficulty realizing that a child has to learn to "read" pictures just as he has to learn how to see the world in the first place. This point is made more clear to us when we occasionally hear of someone who has sight brought to him for the first time in his life or for the first time in many years. One woman at such a time went walking with her seeing-eye dog and was so overwhelmed by what appeared to be trees rushing toward her and pavement rushing under her that she had to close her eyes again and be led along in her familiar way. It took concentration for her to learn how to see the trees and pavement in their proper perspective in relation to herself and other objects.

An infant, too, learns to see things. His explorations

help in this process. When a child begins seeing pictures he has another new world to master. There are a number of skills involved in picture reading. We cannot simply show a preschool child a picture of a camel, for instance, and expect that he will suddenly know what a camel is. Our visual aids do not produce that kind of magic. Those of us who have seen camels only in pictures, yet still feel we know what one looks like, have gained our knowledge by a combination of skills and mental operations. We compare sizes of things. We figure how big a camel is in relation to a man. We compare various features of the camel to other animals we have seen or touched or ridden. But the preschool child lacks our background of knowledge and our ability to do mental operations. He needs a great deal of experience with pictures to learn to read them properly.

There are two schools of thought about the kinds of pictures that are best for young children to learn from. Some people would advise us to use simple pictures of one or only a few objects with no background and a minimum of extra details. Others would advise us to use a full picture with many details. The problem here is that no systematic research has been done that encompasses various ages and various teaching purposes. It would seem better to give children experiences with all kinds of pictures. The simple one object pictures will accomplish some purposes with children, such as their learning to name objects or group objects in certain ways, and the full, detailed pictures will accomplish other purposes, such as their relating things within a picture, and reading a "story" into it.

Simple conversation is one of the best ways to help children learn from a picture. Just talk with them about it. A good first question to ask is, "What do you see?" Then ask, "What else?" and "What else?" until the children have pretty well observed the contents of the picture. Then begin asking questions that require other kinds of thinking. "Do you think the baby bird will like that worm?" "What other foods might the mother bring?" "How do you think the mother knew the baby was hungry?" "Who do you think made this nest?" "What will the bird do when it is bigger?" "Will it find its own food?"

Some pictures you will use to tell a story. After hearing the story once or more, some children can tell you about it. Some pictures you will use for naming, matching and sorting games, which help to develop language. Games for these are given in Chapter 6. Some pictures you will build up piece by piece on a flannelboard. Use pictures in many ways — not just one way.

Sometimes you can draw pictures as the children watch. Announce that you will draw something God made, then draw a tree or flower or butterfly, and let the children guess. Draw a series of things we need and ask what we need each for — a glass of water to drink, bread to eat, a lamp to see, a door to go in. This series can end with a picture of Jesus which you may show ready-made, instead of drawing. What do we need Jesus for? To give life.

Sometimes you can make "living pictures" to match a printed picture. Use flannelgraph figures for this and you will find it easy to adapt to any level of difficulty. Place Mary on the board and have a child come up and be Mary. Add Joseph and have another child be Joseph. Help the remaining children see the flannelgraph Mary and Joseph, and the other Mary and Joseph. Add shepherds or Simeon and Anna. After experience with making living pictures you can let your children do more and more of the planning. Let them study the picture you make on the board and try to duplicate it off the board.

Images. Images are the pictures we form in our minds—mental images representing real happenings or imaginary happenings, true to life or distorted. They are another of the symbols we need as fuel for thinking and, contrary to a popular notion, children are not naturally more adept at this than adults. They need to learn this skill just as any other. A wide experience with life itself is the best way to develop this skill.

Pictures, visualized stories, picture book stories, and other classroom activities help to extend life experience. When children are older it is sometimes good to have stories without visuals so they can use and develop their ability to internalize and form their own mental images. But at the preschool period this ability is not well developed and you probably will want stories visualized most of the time.

The kinesthetic or movement and feeling sense is an important avenue for perceiving images and coming to internalize them. Teachers make use of the kinesthetic sense in the many movement activities common to preschool classrooms. As children play the story, pretend to be a growing tree, form a sun with their arms, and so forth, they are sensing through their bodies. Position, movement, tension and other sensations are perceived through nerve end organs of muscles, tendons and joints. The living pictures activity described above uses a combination of visual and kinesthetic senses to help develop internal images of the pictures. Such a combination suits this age. Children in their early years do a great amount of their learning by the kinesthetic sense and they are growing into a society where "schooling" looms large, and we rely a great deal on the visual and auditory senses. In later life we can see action — say, a tennis game — in either a still or a moving picture and we can internalize it. That is we have a mental image of what it feels like to hit the ball. We can even just hear of the tennis play or other action and still internalize the image more or less accurately, depending on our experience with the particular action.

Preschool children still need much kinesthetic learning to help them internalize images. Experience with real objects is good too. And gradually pictures and words can help extend experience beyond the immediate environment. Coupling the kinesthetic sense with the visual sense — coupling action with pictures — is a useful classroom procedure for this purpose.

Physical Learning

In the ages from 2 to 4 the average child's growth slows. He may grow about five inches during this time and gain about eight pounds.

The child uses this period of life to perfect physical abilities. He outgrows his toddling and perfects his walking. He learns to run with more skill. Probably his most important physical achievement in these years is the perfection of running and walking. He learns to climb with speed and precision. All physical activity is more directed than in the first two years of life.

While the child develops precision with large movements, he is not at the same stage in small movements, such as those required for writing or coloring. This is why it is inappropriate for us to require precision in this kind of work. These are skills which depend more on maturation than on learning. When the time is right the child will learn these things easily. Our best approach is to try to design learning activities to fit the child's present level of development rather than to try to push him on to the next stage of development.

A characteristic of this period is that the child indulges in new abilities for their own sake. When a new word or phrase intrigues him he may practice saying it over and over, seemingly for the pure pleasure of rolling it off his tongue. When using paints, crayons or clay he will do the same thing. The motion — the manipulating —is itself the purpose of the activity.

This is sometimes hard for teachers to adjust to, since our adult view is so oriented toward the finished product. We think the purpose of a classroom activity is to make something, to complete a picture, to model a recognizable object, or some other end product. But the child view is oriented toward the process. He is painting or coloring or smashing. He is sweeping the brush or swinging the crayon or poking the clay. He does gradually become interested in making things and somewhere around age 4 he enters the "representational" stage in his art, where he draws or models representations of people and objects. It is best to let this grow naturally. The child needs plenty of experience with process before centering on the end product. Do not force this stage before its time.

Social-Emotional Learning

Probably the most important learning a child does during his early preschool years is in the social-emotional area. Good emotional development contributes to other kinds of learning. And, on the other hand, the most important result of other learning may be that it contributes to the social-emotional development of the person.

The preschool child is largely an autonomous individual, in the early stages of becoming a social creature. His egocentric world is beginning to open a bit and he is becoming increasingly aware of others.

Although he is not truly sensitive to the needs of others he can be taught in various ways how to respond to others. Group experiences are valuable to the child in this stage of his development.

A child can learn in specific instances how to make another happy. You can reward him for giving a toy to a crying child, or for helping a small child reach something high, or for not pushing someone. Reward him with praise or with a toy for himself or other tangible reward. This may seem to be promoting selfish motives, but it provides a foundation for helping others unselfishly later. You not only need to reward often, but you also need to provide ideas of how to help another. Each specific incident as it comes along is a learning experience that the child can understand, whereas he cannot understand general admonitions to be nice to others, or to share with others.

Talk about the various children in your class. Help them learn each other's names and learn things about each other. Keep assuring children that the others are friends.

Give opportunities for the children to do things together—not cooperatively, as that is not entirely possible, but collectively. When playing the story, everyone is Joseph looking for the brothers, or everyone is Noah building the boat. When making murals everyone pastes on sheep. Use simple, teacher-directed games.

The child not only needs to learn how to manage his relationships with others, he also needs to learn how to manage himself. As he tests his abilities he frequently overreaches himself, and becomes angry or frustrated. You can help by providing some routine and order in your class. The child can adjust to routine, and it reduces the number of decisions he must make, thus reducing the frequency of his frustrations. Temper tantrums are quite normal during these years and usually the best way to handle these is to ignore them. Show indifference to this kind of behavior, but shower praise and attention on acceptable social behavior.

Children need wise and patient guidance through these years of learning to become socialized beings and developing the foundation of Christian character and personality. You can look upon these aspects of development as a more important part of your work than the cognitive learnings that may happen in your classroom.

READING CHECK

1. If a child learns about God too early he is likely to grow up with a distorted idea of God.   T   F
2. It is impossible to make the concept of prayer concrete enough for most preschoolers to understand. T   F
3. Good and evil are among the simpler concepts to teach.   T   F
4. Three major kinds of symbols children acquire in their early years are words, pictures and mental images.
                                                                                                                        T   F
5. Children do not need to fully understand a Bible verse or a song before learning it.   T   F
6. There are complicated skills involved in reading pictures.   T   F
7. Preschool children generally have more imagination than adults.   T   F
8. No important developmental gains accrue from trying to teach children to color within lines.   T   F
9. A child's social-emotional learning is not as important as his cognitive learning.   T   F

Answers: 1—F, 2—F, 3—F, 4—T, 5—T, 6—T, 7—F, 8—T, 9—F

3 What Handwork Can Children Do?

At times you may be enticed to search for an exotic handcraft idea, and you may feel a workshop was successful if you came home with a "cute" new idea. Now, cute ideas add spice to your teaching life, and you can use a little of that, but what you need for your long succession of classes week after week is to know how to handle a few basics.

If your projects require cutting, folding, assembling with brads, or other complicated procedures you usually will end up doing them yourself. The way out of that common plight is to become familiar with the abilities of young preschool children, and with your children in particular. You need to know not only what handwork skills they now have, but also what skills you may reasonably expect to teach them. Master the use of the basic skills which follow and you will find they take care of most of your handwork needs.

Coloring

In alphabetical order, coloring comes first. In popularity and traditional use, it also far outstrips any other kind of handwork. Whether or not coloring should have such a prominent place is an interesting question. Some teachers feel it is "educational" for children to color pictures. They believe that it is good for children to learn to do neat work and stay within the lines, and that they learn Bible content in this way. Other teachers believe children cannot think about Bible content while they are thinking about staying within lines. Some also believe that children's muscular and neural development is not yet conducive to such exacting work. And art teachers are concerned that children's creativity may be stifled in this way.

You may find that you are on one side of this question, and your children's parents or weekday preschool teachers on the other side. And your children will vary widely. Some will already have been taught to color carefully within the lines, and some will seem never to have met a coloring picture. A helpful attitude for you to take in the midst of all this is to realize that coloring itself is not such an important part of your Bible lesson. No child is going to learn how to love the Lord or live the Christian life better because of it. No parent is going to come to the Lord because you make sure his child's paper is skillfully colored.

You can emphasize things more important than coloring skill. Talk about a picture with your children and help them talk about it too. Children can learn to say any new words involved. Some can learn to tell the story that goes with the picture. After this preparation, let the children color as they will, from scribble-coloring to fill-in style.

At this point in the class session, you should think more about the children than about their pictures. Let the children enjoy their work. Help them gain confidence. Don't criticize and goad them to color this part or that part, to use green instead of brown, and so forth. Don't use this as a time to teach "sharing," but have enough crayons for everyone. Appreciate the children's work in a genuine, not gushy, manner.

For a change from crayons, sometimes you can try

other mediums. Children love to use felt pens because of the brilliant colors they produce. Chalk allows opportunity to blend colors. Wetting the chalk or the paper provides still another effect. Sometimes give the children blank paper instead of pictures.

Some preschool children can learn to make crayon rubbings. For rubbings you tape a small cardboard pattern to a table. The child learns to tape a sheet of paper to the table over the pattern, and to rub with the side of a peeled crayon. This is something children have not usually done at home, so you may need to repeat the project three or four times before the children gain skill enough to do this well.

Drawing

This category is included more to tell what children cannot do than what they can do. The information here will save you—and your children—from a class where you hand them blank paper and say, "Draw a picture of today's story." This would be fine for primary children, but not for young preschoolers.

A brief summary here of a child's developmental sequence in drawing will help you understand what you observe among your own children.

1. Scribble stage. Exploratory manipulation of muscles and crayon or pencil.
2. Recognition stage. Child "sees" something in his scribbles. The first one is usually a circular shape which he sees as a person. He draws first and names his drawing afterward.
3. Representational stage. Child can name what he will draw before drawing it. His first drawings are usually circles with appendages to make tadpole-like people. From here he advances to more and more mature representations of objects he wishes to draw.

When you understand the sequence of development in drawing, and when you have observed where your own children are in this sequence, then you will not ask the impossible. Actually, you will do very little drawing in your preschool classes. The best kind is what children spontaneously produce on their own.

But occasionally you will find a directed drawing lesson to be useful. You can use the demonstration method. Ask, "Want to see me draw a tree?" Then show how you scribble a treetop, and how you put a trunk on your tree. Keep your drawing super simple, and children can be encouraged to do what you did.

Manipulating

This is a broad category that includes water play, sand play, puzzles and other items to fit, sort, string, and manipulate in various ways. It can also include kneading bread, decorating cookies and numerous other activities which teachers bring into classrooms to enliven them and to help children learn from real things.

Clay, or play dough, is often the teacher's best friend. When your children have listened for as long as you can hold their attention, and when they begin pushing one another and in other ways showing their restlessness, you can get out the clay.

What can little childen do with clay? Their abilities here are somewhat parallel to the sequence described previously under "Drawing." That is, if children have not yet reached the representational stage you cannot expect them to model people and objects at will. Sometimes a child will form something and then announce what it is, but this is different from deciding first to make something and then forming it.

The most useful thing you can do with such young children is to help them learn various ways to manipulate clay. Sit with them and work a piece of clay yourself. Talk about what the children are doing. "Look, Danny is rolling his long and thin." "Jill poked a big hole." When the children run out of ideas, insert a few yourself. You can smash, pull, stretch, fold, pile, form balls, break, join together. You can make flat, round, long, short, pointed. You can poke two eyes and say, "Look, I made a face." It could be a sheep's face or a man's face or whatever goes with your lesson. Cut cookies with plastic bottle tops. Make prints by pressing in items of any interesting shape.

The plasticene which is usually sold in variety stores is too stiff for young children to use easily. The following recipe makes an entirely satisfactory play dough. It will keep for several months if stored in an airtight container.

> 1½ cups flour (not self-rising)
> 1 cup salt
> 1 tablespoon powdered alum
> 1 tablespoon vegetable oil
> 1 cup boiling water
> food coloring

Mix dry ingredients. Add oil and boiling water. Stir vigorously until well blended. Add coloring and knead until evenly tinted.

Here is the developmental sequence a child passes through in learning to work with modeling materials.

1. Child manipulates—beats, pounds—in an exploratory manner.
2. With conscious control, child rolls, breaks, and tries other manipulations. Sometimes names a product he has made.
3. Child can announce beforehand what he will make. Increasing ability to pull out or add on details, such as nose and legs.

Sand play, along with water play, is a natural, basic kind of activity for young children. Before preschools were ever invented, children were learning about their world by playing with the sand, dirt and water around them.

The ideal place for sand is outdoors. But many teachers have figured out ways to handle it indoors too. Usually their system involves a box set in the center of the room, which makes it easier to sweep and clean up spilled sand. A large box for several children to play with at once, may look like this.

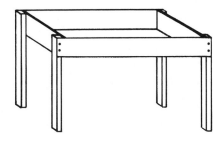

A small box for about two children at a time may look like this.

Instead of sand, some preschools use cornmeal. This is easier on floor surfaces if it gets spilled. Wheat, bird seed of various kinds, and even small beans have been used by teachers who are creative at finding surplus or rejected materials from local industries or farms.

A sandbox can be used as a story telling visual. Many Bible stories lend themselves to this medium, for example, Mary and Joseph traveling to Bethlehem, or the family traveling to Egypt.

After you have told a story, the children can sometimes do the story themselves—or part of it. But, as with all play, sand play will soon go the children's own way; they will not stay long with the story structure you may have given them. For their own experimentations with sand, children will make good use of spoons, shovels, sticks, pieces of pipe or hose, sieves and other tools you provide. They can use all kinds of containers for filling, pouring, sprinkling, and so forth. Have lids for some of the containers. Put holes in some of them.

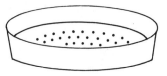

Holes in the top for sprinkling.

Holes in the bottom for sifting out.

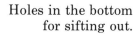

Holes in the side for accidents.

Holes on both ends
for a funnel or
non-fillable bottle.

Josh was a boy who got so intrigued with the small sandbox in his Sunday school room that for several weeks the teacher could not lure him away to story time or any other activity. If someone had been including Josh in attention span research, he would have recorded each week one full hour of uninterrupted attention to his own researches in the sand. During this time Josh looked forward to going to Sunday school. He always had a happy greeting and a happy goodbye for his teacher.

After several weeks, whatever need the sandbox fulfilled in Josh's development was finally satisfied, and Josh began entering into other activities in the classroom. We don't always know what the children are learning, but when they are so fully engrossed in their activities we can be sure something important is happening.

Vocabulary learning can accompany sand play, and a perceptive teacher can enhance this by entering into conversation with the children. Words of direction and position are particularly important in understanding stories, and these are experienced in concrete form in the sandbox. Up, down, over there, across, around, under, part way, to, away—these and similar terms can be heard, experienced and spoken at the sandbox. Empty, full, pour, spill, leak and other words concerned with physics are also learned.

Water play can be set up in a similar way. Sometimes the box is built like the stand-up sandbox shown earlier, but it is lined with zinc or plastic, and has a drain hole added. Or smaller tubs and dishpans can be used on tables or on the floor.

With water available, you can let your children bathe baby Samuel or other Bible babies. They can float Noah's ark or float fishing boats on the Sea of Galilee. But, of course, they will proceed to their own devices just as with the sand. All the same kinds of tools and containers suggested for sand will be useful also in water play, and a few more can be added. Soap, bubble pipes, and straws for blowing; sponges, wash cloths; pieces of cork, styrofoam and other items that float; items that sink; pitchers with pouring spouts, plastic dishes and other house play items—the list is almost endless. Sometimes provide brushes and paint with water. Paint walls, steps, or sidewalks. Watch the paint dry.

Have plastic aprons for the children to wear, and have towels and a mop for wipe-up. Show the children how to pour, wring their sponges and so forth over the tub and not over the floor. If you feel you cannot handle the mess of water play, try letting just one or two children participate at a time.

Puzzles are extremely popular, and always good activity for the children. Nature pictures and Bible pictures are best for use in churches. It probably is not a good idea to mix in Little Bo Peep or Ernie or other secular topics. Children should learn to associate certain stories and characters with the Sunday school classroom.

Sturdy, wooden puzzles with set-in pieces are best for this age. Therefore it is difficult to make very satisfactory homemade puzzles. A puzzle rack for storing each puzzle on its individual shelf is invaluable for keeping all the pieces in order.

For homemade items you will have much better success with sewing cards. Commercial cards are usually rectangular in shape, with the pictures—and sewing holes—set within the rectangle. But young children have an easier time sewing if the holes are all around the edge, so your handmade cards can be planned this way, and will be superior to store cards for your classroom.

Make simple outline pictures of trees or any item God made, or of Samuel's coat or other Bible item. Mount your pictures onto cardboard, and punch holes an inch or two apart all around the edge. At one hole tie a piece of yarn for sewing. Stiffen the other tip of the yarn by wrapping a piece of Scotch tape around it. The tape will act as a needle for poking through the sewing holes. These cards, of course, can be reused many times; simply pull out the yarn one child has sewn and the card is ready for the next child. Shoestrings also work for sewing, as do blunt rug needles.

For stringing, you will also need yarn with an end stiffened with tape. Tie a bead or macaroni at the other end. You can buy wooden or plastic beads for stringing. Or use Cheerios, Fruit Loops, macaroni, or short pieces of plastic straws. People in Bible times made the tabernacle and the temple look pretty with their handwork. Your children can hang their pretty strings to decorate their church. Or if they can't bear to leave them, they can wear the strings around their necks when they go home.

Another easy-to-make manipulative item is a sorting set. Use egg cartons for the sorting cups, and collect beans and macaroni, or buttons and beads for sorting. Children can practice sorting by color or size or type.

With a variety of manipulative items, you won't have to always have puzzles—or any one activity—for those who arrive early. Children will enjoy the variety and so will you.

Painting

Painting takes more preparation and equipment than crayoning, but it is worth the extra work. With paint a child can easily make broad strokes of brilliant color, and that is more satisfying than pressing hard with a crayon to get a lesser stroke of color. A child engrossed in painting will often do sheet after sheet. Sometime you can teach "God made blue." You probably have taught that God made trees or God made flowers. Try "God made blue." The children can paint blue, and you can admire all their individual blues — the light or dark, the streaky or wavy or spotty, the smooth or bumpy. You can fill a bulletin board or wall with their blue and all stand back to admire it.

One color at a time is all these children need for painting. Use poster paints, not pale water colors. Pour each child only a small amount of paint, then he cannot dip his brush handle into it, but only the tip of the brush. This one hint alone is worth the price of this book, because when paint gets on the handles it soon is on the hands, and when it is on hands it soon is on everything else. If you set up painting to be a neat operation and guide your children carefully into the procedure, they will surprise you with the way they manage it.

Use large brushes with handles only about six inches long. You probably will have to cut off handles to arrange this; it is a mystery why brush manufacturers think children need long, unmanageable handles. An inexpensive substitute for brushes is sponge squares with clothespin handles. You will need, also, some paint shirts. Old shirts or blouses do nicely. Cut sleeves short. Button or pin at the back. Simple capes could be made by cutting neck holes in the centers of pieces of plastic or other material.

Paper to paint on need not be expensive. Ask around your church for available used paper. Children can paint on the back side of used paper—or on the used side. They will even enjoy painting on newspaper. Children do not need easels; they can stand or sit at a table, or they may kneel on the floor to paint.

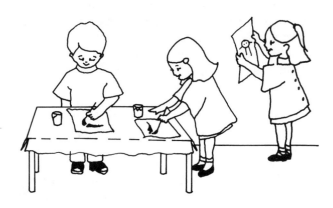

So the materials to collect are: paint, small cans or jars to use as individual paint containers, brushes, paint shirts and paper. Now, the next problem is how to manage all this in the classroom. And the best solution is to teach the children to manage it themselves. Arrange everything where the children can get them. Open shelves are good, but if you lack that advantage you can at least set your boxes of supplies down within reach. A child can get paper, brush, and paint can to set at his place. He can get a paint shirt and try to put it on. He may need your help with this. And when he is all ready, you pour him a bit of paint. Simple? When it works smoothly it really is quite simple. But of course it is your careful teaching that makes it so. You need to know when to help children and when not to help, and when to encourage a child to just a bit more self-sufficiency.

After a child finishes a paper, he can take it to your

designated "drying spot"—perhaps along the edge of the floor. Or if it is too drippy you may wish to do this yourself. Then the child gets himself another sheet. Never limit children to one sheet of paper. A famous book illustrator remembers fondly the one art teacher in his school life who allowed him two sheets of paper. There is no reason in our times to be so niggardly with paper, and there certainly is nothing gained by it.

Plan your clean-up procedure just as carefully as the rest. Where should the children put their paint-soaked brushes? In a large can? Teach the children each procedure at the time they need it; they will not remember if you try to teach it all ahead of time, but they will remember after they go through the procedure once or twice.

An alternate way to manage painting in the classroom is to set up just one or two painting places, and let the children take turns. Sometimes you might try finger painting, either on sheets of paper, or confined in a jelly roll pan. Some children enjoy the mess of finger painting, and others prefer to keep their hands clean.

Developmental sequence in painting proceeds as follows:

1. Child uses paint to explore. Spreads paint and lays paint over paint.
2. Lines and circles appear, then other forms and blocks of color. Later, child sometimes names what he has made.
3. Child can announce beforehand what he will paint. Conscious control of his forms.

Pasting

Like painting, children can manage this if you have suitable materials and teach appropriate procedure. First, you will need either glue or soft paste. Give each child a bit on a piece of paper or small container, and see that each child has his own paste brush. Brushes may be hard to find, but keep asking for them at your local stores; they are much easier to use than spreaders. And glue bottles are impossible; don't expect children to manage these. Rather than individual size glue bottles for children it is better to get one giant size, arm yourself with a pair of pliers for opening it, and pour out each week what you need. And you just never know what other uses you will find for those pliers in your purse.

Teach the children to brush paste to the back of the piece to be pasted down, and then to set it in place and press. Never put paste on the main paper. Young children cannot gauge how far to spread the paste and you will find the latter method much messier. Putting paste only on the smaller piece is far neater, and children have no trouble doing it this way.

Since children can paste, or enjoy learning to paste, you will want to look for ways to make a real activity of this. Just to paste a picture onto a sheet of paper does not make an activity, but to paste colored-paper flowers all over the paper to make a picture *is* an activity. Design your pasting projects to be collage style whenever possible and see how quickly your children become expert pasters—most of them at least.

Sometimes you can do a group pasting project. Place a large sheet of paper on the wall and let the children paste items on it to form a mural. Plan something that is loosely organized, then you can relax about where children paste things. For instance, your mural can be a sky and the children paste on stars. Or the mural can be a pasture and the children paste on sheep. Put up a picture of Jesus and let your class paste children around Him. Draw a large tree and let the children paste on leaves. Flowers in a field, animals about the ark, fish in the water, birds in the sky—all these are mural possibilities.

This kind of group project is a little like parallel play—the children are not really cooperating, but they are working alongside each other on the same thing. Any mural you plan will have to fit this developmental level of the children.

You will usually have to cut out the items for pasting yourself, so look for time-saving ways to do this. When cutting pictures of children from a mail-order catalog, cut in rough rectangular shapes and do not take time to carefully cut around the figures. Use the same method when cutting flowers or vegetables from a seed-catalog. If you use a pattern or draw your own shape, pile up several sheets of paper, use heavy scissors, and cut several at a time. Sometimes your older children will want to try cutting their own items—especially something like leaves, where almost any shape will do.

Mural backgrounds can be from large rolls of art paper or any kind of large paper you have available. Even newspaper—the already printed kind—will do. Children pay no attention to the print and are just as happy pasting on newspaper as they are painting on it.

Here is a recipe for homemade paste, which can be kept soft to work easily with paste brushes.

½ cup flour
½ cup sugar
½ cup cold water
2 cups boiling water
1½ teaspoons powdered alum
¼ teaspoon oil of wintergreen (preservative)

Mix first three ingredients. Slowly add boiling water, stirring until thick and clear. Remove from heat, add alum and mix well. Add oil of wintergreen if paste is not to be used immediately. Store in tight jar. This can be thinned with hot water if it gets too thick.

Other Handwork Skills

The skills already discussed are the basic ones which you can profitably use over and over, but they do not encompass the full range of possibilities. Sometimes published lessons make use of stickers, which are within the abilities of most young children. Occasionally you will have Easter seals or similar stickers left over, and rather than throwing them out you could take them to your classroom. As with pasting, it is easier if the children can place stickers almost anywhere—flowers in a field, stars in a sky, and so forth. But from time to time you can have a more exacting project where a sticker needs to go in a certain place.

Cutting with scissors is not a skill that most preschool children can do successfully, and it is best left to the kindergarten department. Cutting is like coloring within the lines, in that it depends so largely on physical maturation. When a child is physically mature enough to manage this job he will learn it quickly and easily. When he is not yet mature enough, he will struggle and learn slowly and experience frustration, so it is better to wait for the right time.

Since the right time comes at different ages for different children, you may want to have scissors available for children to use as a matter of free choice. Sometimes you can plan projects on several levels. For instance, if the children are pasting leaves on a tree, some could paste precut leaves which you have prepared and others could cut their own. If you are not particular about the shapes the children will not be either, and they will be happy with their work.

The last few weeks before children are promoted into the kindergarten department you may wish to provide special cutting practice, and encourage those who have not yet learned how. This will help them to do the handwork which is found in kindergarten lesson books. Don't forget to have left-handed scissors for any children who need them.

Folding is another skill that does not find its best place in the preschool classroom. If you have projects which require folding, you should do this for the children before class. Brads, staples, cutting slits and assembling pieces of paper all fall into this category too.

For a change from pasting, sometimes the children enjoy using tape. This is a little like using stickers. You probably will have to tear off pieces of tape and put them on the children's thumbs or the table edge. Then the children can tape their leaves to the mural tree instead of pasting them. With this system you could try using a bare branch and make a three-dimensional tree. With the branch tree, children could tape paper birds to pieces of yarn and then drape yarn over the branches to make a tree full of birds.

There probably is no end to the original ideas you could bring to your class, and it is good to be different from time to time, but the basic skills of coloring, painting, pasting, and manipulating clay and other items will provide the core of your handwork program.

Values of Handwork

We should ask the question of why we have handwork in church preschool programs, and we should give a thoughtful answer. Many times handwork is justified by repeating a maxim that "children learn by doing," or another maxim that "after the children hear the lesson, then they need to apply it." There is some truth in these maxims, but they do not adequately justify handwork—art work.

In a lesson about Samuel helping, there are many ways a teacher can have her children "do" the lesson. They can play the ways Samuel helped, and they can play ways they can help both at home and in the classroom. They can sing about helping, talk about helping, look at pictures about helping. They can play games that reinforce the idea. They can make plans for helping in a particular situation. In comparison with some of the above activities, coloring a picture of Samuel helping comes out as rather a second best. It is not close to "doing" the lesson, and it is quite far from "applying" the lesson.

But there are other ways to justify coloring a picture of Samuel. Some of the values in pictures themselves, as discussed in Chapter 2, will apply here. They apply whether the Samuel picture is crayoned, or painted, or textured by pasting fabric on his robe. And the profit comes not only in class where teacher and pupils talk about the picture and work on it, but it also comes later at home where the child and parent can talk about the picture again. This take-home feature is what many teachers feel is most valuable about the lesson-related handwork the children do.

Beyond the picture or other product of handwork, there are still other values from the process of doing the work. These values are probably more far reaching, having more effect on the child. Art experiences provide the child with opportunities to explore, experiment, and express ideas about himself and the world around him. He can express feelings and learn to handle them—feelings that he often is not able to handle with words, because of his limited vocabulary. Art strengthens the child's ability to observe and to image the people and the world around him. It increases his sensitivity to others. Art involves assuming responsibility for choosing, even if it is only choosing which color to use, but better if he can sometimes choose which materials to use. Then he must do something with his choices, exercise judgment and control. He gains success experiences which help build a good concept of self.

When children work together there also is social growth. A child becomes more aware of others working alongside him and more sensitive to their opinions and needs and their property. There is intellectual growth as the child invents new ways to use his materials and tries out new forms and methods. When he wants to talk about his work he finds need for more words. There is physical development in the developing muscular control and motor coordination and the neurological eye and hand coordination. And there is growth in the art skills themselves, all of which, in turn, contribute to the child's self-confidence.

There are many values in handwork, and these are not limited to the paper-type projects that are usually labeled handwork in preschool classes. The same things could be said about sandbox play, block play and many other activities. Probably the reason paper handwork is used more than the others is that it is easier to design it so it seems lesson-related to the teacher. That value is given a higher priority in church programs than some of the others.

Another justification of handwork in preschool classrooms is that it simply is difficult to carry on a program of verbal learning for an hour or more. In older age groups the teaching can make more and more use of words and the ideas they convey. But with young children this is not so easy. One job the children have at this stage is to acquire words, and after the stories, games and rhymes have done their part, teachers turn to handwork to finish out the hour with another kind of learning.

Though it is not essential to have handwork in every session, there are many reasons to give it a prominent place in our Christian education programs.

READING CHECK

1. The ability to color neatly within the lines depends mostly on
   a. practice.
   b. teaching.
   c. maturation.

2. The most advanced of these stages of drawing is the
   a. scribble stage.
   b. representational stage.
   c. recognition stage.

3. Which is the most difficult for a young child?
   a. using scissors.
   b. using clay.
   c. using paint.

4. When making murals you should let the children
   a. plan their own.
   b. work in committees on different parts.
   c. all paste on the same kind of things.

5. Handwork period is when children are
   a. learning most intensely.
   b. growing in many ways.
   c. applying the lesson to their lives.

Answers: 1—c, 2—b, 3—a, 4—c, 5—b

4 What about Music and Rhymes?

Music, rhymes, rhythm—these are an almost natural way to teach. Children who are at the nursery rhyme stage of growth can be reached by a nursery rhyme approach in the church. Some of this is fun and nonsense, but fun can be learning, and nonsense has its uses too; so enter the world of childhood on this bouncing, rhythmic path.

Rhymes

One of the main jobs preschoolers have is learning language. Nursery rhymes help them do this. Rhyming words, alliteration, repetition, rhythm, all attract children. They listen and mimic, and practice their language skills: phonics and grammar and vocabulary.

And beyond those serious, academic learnings is a much higher learning—about communication and literature, about what it means to be human, about experiencing the world around us, about thinking of God. Poems are sometimes described as being more than the sum of their words. While nursery rhymes may not qualify as poems, they too are more than the sum of their words. They project feelings and moods and meaning beyond the mere words. Imagine the effect of "Soft Things" on a group of little children. (Rhymes and songs are given in the latter part of this chapter.)

Rhymes are for individuals and for groups. A child at play may be heard rolling off his tongue a word or a line he has heard or a full rhyme he has learned. And a child enjoying a rhyme with a group is being drawn a bit more into the community of people; it is another step on the road from egocentric individualism to full membership in the society of humans.

Rhymes with motions are not limited to fingers. *Action rhymes* is a better name for these than *fingerplays* because this name describes more of the rhymes. In group teaching, action rhymes are most commonly used along with a story time. They provide the warm-up, or they provide variety and transition between stories, or occasionally they provide a reinforcement, being a rhyme version of the story just read. "Jesus Went Up" is an example of a rhyme which may be used along with the Bible story on this topic.

Every teacher should have at least a few action rhymes memorized, and others available on handy cards. The memorized rhymes will help you rescue lagging attention or head off an impending disturbance. On such occasions you have no time to reach for your cards and shuffle through them looking for an appropriate rhyme. "Open, Shut Them" is a rhyme that almost every preschool teacher uses from time to time. "Two Little Hands," "Fee, Fie, Fo, Fum" and many others will serve the same purposes.

Younger preschool children have trouble doing two things at once, such as making motions and saying words. Some of these children will say the words and some will do the motions. Some may do neither one for a time. These variations need not worry you; you can safely let each child participate in his own way.

Sometimes use finger puppets or hand puppets with rhymes. Let children take turns wearing a puppet as all the children repeat the lines it says.

Songs

Teachers write their lesson publishers for help. "My children don't sing," they say; or "My children can't sing"; or the even more frustrated, "My children refuse to sing."

The only answer is, "Sing anyway." We must remember that little children are beginners in music. We have sung our choruses and hymns in the pews, around campfires, by the kitchen sink. Or it might have been the hit tunes or other songs. We sang them on school busses, hummed along with the shopping music, or working music, or eating music. We turn on music as we drive. We are far from beginners in music, yet we must reach the children who are.

You are the preschool teacher—perhaps the first teacher your children have ever had. So don't expect your children to come to you skilled at singing. You are the one starting them out on the road toward enjoying music and praising God through song. Don't abdicate because your children don't sing well yet. Those who just sit through a group singing time are learning. They are being exposed to music, and in their own good time they will begin to participate too. You should sing even if you are the only one singing. Don't be scared off by your possible lack of musical training—you have had more of this than you think, as indicated earlier. Anyone who can sing "Happy Birthday" is skillful enough to teach music to preschoolers.

You can use familiar tunes such as "Mary Had a Little Lamb" or "Farmer in the Dell," and make up words for almost any idea you wish to teach. Learn the "Children's Chant" tune; children can sing this earlier than any other tune, and you can find numerous uses for it. A few folk songs, such as "Clap Your Hands" add another dimension to your repertoire. You will naturally use the most-beloved Sunday school song of all—"Jesus Loves Me"—and its companion, "Jesus Loves the Little Children." These songs are more difficult than special nursery level songs, but they are classics and children can grow into them. Instead of singing in the latter song about all the races of the world, at this age try singing about all the children of our class. Squeeze in as many names as needed in the middle of this song; your children will not mind the loss of rhythm at all. They love to hear their names in a song, so learn the trick of putting children's names in many songs—in "Where Is Thumbkin?" for instance. Learn "Sally Wore a Yellow Dress" or a similar song that is designed for the purpose of singing about individual children in the class.

When you use songs for teaching Bible thoughts, be sure they make straightforward statements that children can understand. Notice the difference between the Bible song suggested in this chapter, and the familiar "B-I-B-L-E" which is meant for older children. One says, "I will love the Bible," and one says, "I stand alone on the Word of God." This second song uses the word *stand* in a non-concrete meaning which preschoolers cannot comprehend, and the word *alone* is ambiguous. Is it I who am alone, or is it the Word of God? All this, which seems so simple to us, is beyond the minds of your little beginners in life and language.

Puppets work well with songs, just as they do with rhymes. Let a child stand in front and wear a finger

puppet of the sun while everyone sings "God made the sun." Another child wears a finger puppet of the moon while everyone sings "God made the moon." Have a finger puppet or hand puppet of a child. Someone can wear it while all sing "Jesus Loves Me." The possibilities are endless. Some children will actually particpate better in singing if they are singing for a puppet instead of for themselves.

Children sometimes make up songs of their own. As they play or work, various ones may sing a phrase or two about what they are doing or perhaps about something they heard earlier in class. If such happy events occur in your class, treat these as real songs. You can join in the singing with a child. If she sings, "I'm painting re-ed," you can answer, "Susie made a so-ong." Sometimes you can write down the child's song and use it later in a group time. Introduce it to all the children as Susie's song or Gary's song. You never need to feel that you should help your children graduate from their own songs to the "real" songs you offer them. Their songs are more real to them than the ones you get from a book. Such music is from the heart and from the understanding. Encourage it.

What about children's singing range? Some books in the past have specified enormously wide ranges for young children—extending higher than most teachers like to sing. While it is true that children are able to reach higher tones, they seldom do so in a song. You will have greater success if you keep most of your songs within a short range and pitch them on the lower half of the staff, extending from about middle C or D to A above them. This is a comfortable range for most women with untrained voices, so it is good news for many teachers who have felt themselves unqualified to teach singing.

Most young preschoolers do not actually "carry a tune," as we express it. Occasionally you will have an unusual child or two who do actually sing through whole tunes. Other children will approximate the tunes, being on pitch at times on some of the phrases, and off pitch at other times. But you need to sing anyway. It is by much practice and much exposure to singing that children grow in this ability.

Songs with a limited range are easier for the children. Their own natural tunes, such as the first line of the "Children's Chant" tune, encompass only three or four notes. Traditional tunes such as "Mulberry Bush" and "Farmer in the Dell" use only five or six notes. These singable tunes of limited range are the ones children will master first. The song "Jesus Loves Me" and some of the folk tunes you will use extend the range to about eight notes. Preschoolers cannot sing these as easily as the five-note songs. Songs beyond the five to eight note range are not recommended for preschool use.

There can be no hard and fast rule about choosing songs for young children. But, in general, the children will sing better on songs which have a narrower range and which are pitched in the lower half of the treble staff. The songs also should have simple word patterns and repetition which can be easily learned.

Never encourage shouting or loud singing; just accept the normal singing volume of those who participate and accept the listening behavior of those who are not yet ready to sing with you.

TEACHING PRESCHOOLERS

Below is the developmental sequence of a young child on his way to group singing. Most of your children will fall somewhere from 1 to 5 on this list, and as you work with them each child can move farther along in his development. Step 5 is not reached by the majority of children in a preschool or nursery class, so you need to see this list as showing the direction the children are heading and not as a sequence of steps which all must complete.

1. Listens to teacher and others sing; sings spontaneously while playing.
2. Joins in actions as a song is sung.
3. Joins on occasional words and phrases.
4. Sings with the group but may not always be in time (sometimes a phrase behind) and may not use the same words.
5. Sings with the group, matching many of the tones.

Rhythm Instruments

With rhythm, as with singing, you need not wait until the children gain skill and accuracy; you need to provide experiences by which the children can grow in their abilities. The key always in these matters is to be concerned with the children and their development rather than with the product of their efforts. You are not arranging rhythm and music displays for parents and others to admire, but you are helping little children learn to enjoy God's gift of music, and learn to praise Him with it. Become as a little child in this, and join the fun along with your class.

Young preschoolers can enjoy music together in a group, but you must remember it is not the cooperative kind of group found in older children's classes. It is more like the parallel play that psychologists and teachers observe in the young. Each child is doing his own thing but he does it alongside the other children. For this reason you will not want any complicated arrangements—not one side playing on the first line and another side playing on the next line, but everyone together doing the same thing.

You can pass out any simple sound-producing instruments and let the children beat or shake as a song is sung. When you first try this you are likely to be the only one singing, since the children will be so busy with their instruments they will forget to sing. They have difficulty doing two things at once. So you can do a song several times; sometimes they can sing and sometimes they can play. They can experience the song in two different dimensions, and it will be more fully theirs than if they only experienced it in one.

Homemade instruments are entirely adequate. Try obtaining from your druggist a number of plastic pill bottles. Put a few beans or other small items in each, and you have a set of shakers. Collect some small boxes; use them without lids or cut away a large part of the tops of the lids; and stretch rubber bands across the openings and around the boxes. This makes a set of harps. Pairs of sticks about eight inches long can be made from dowel rods or any suitable material you are able to get.

With shakers, harps, and sticks you will have a fine variety. You need use them only one at a time. Sometimes use harps with a lullaby and notice the quiet sound that will help the baby sleep. Use sticks with another song. Try to tap them like pretty music, and don't bang them too loud. Sing the song without sticks, then do it again with sticks. Perhaps you won't use shakers at all this week, but save them for another week. Sometimes let the children choose which instrument to use. If you have access to bells, xylophones, drums, and other types of instruments you can work them into your music program too.

If you have space enough and can stand the noise, set up a music center where children individually can experiment with instruments. Set out one or two each of the various instruments you have and let the children use them in their own way. Have a cassette player and short music tapes. Sometimes the children will accompany the music with their instruments. Remember, your pleasure in music will be contagious among your children.

Here is the developmental sequence of a child's use of instruments. As with the singing sequence, you cannot expect your children all to reach step 3, but you can expect them all to advance some along the sequence while they are in your class.

1. Manipulates and experiments with instruments and "makes noise."
2. Accompanies movement or music, but not necessarily in time.
3. Plays along with a group and can keep the tempo much of the time.

Body Rhythms and Sounds

Practically everyone uses one kind of body rhythm—clapping. With a little imagination you can add other kinds of body rhythms or sounds to many stories or songs. If someone in the story is walking try clapping hands on laps to make a walking sound. Or do it faster for a running sound. Pound feet on the floor to make camels come or make a storm come. Tap fingers on the table or floor to make rain. Whoosh air through teeth to make wind.

Motions which go with action rhymes are a type of body rhythm. A more informal type is the motions that often go with playing the story. When the elephant walks to the ark he lumbers along with his trunk (both arms hanging with hands clasped together) waving back and forth. When the frog goes, he hops rhythmically along saying, "Ribet, ribet, ribet."

Children can be raindrops, flying sparrows, and

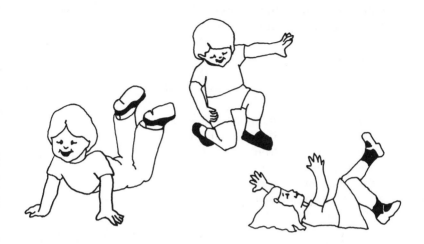

numerous other objects. Sometimes it will be in a play-the-story activity, sometimes with a rhyme, and sometimes with an action song. When you allow movement in the classroom you are allowing the children to be children.

A Beginning Repertoire

You can hardly make it in a preschool classroom without knowing at least a couple of rhymes and a couple of songs. You will need at least a minimum repertoire to begin with and you can build that up gradually as you work along with the children.

The rhymes or songs you do not memorize, but want to use, can be copied on cards. These are handy to place on your lap where you can glance at them as necessary, but still have your hands free to do the motions.

Following, are some useful and much beloved songs and rhymes which you can choose from to start building your own repertoire.

Get ready for a Bible story or other listening experience with one of these. In the rhyme "In the Bible" substitute the names Samuel, David, or anyone else as needed to go with your lesson.

OPEN, SHUT THEM

Open, SHUT them,
Open, SHUT them,
GIVE a little CLAP.

Open, SHUT them,
Open, SHUT them,
LAY them in your LAP.

FEE, FIE, FO, FUM

FEE, FIE, FO, FUM.
SEE my FINGer,
SEE my THUMB.
FEE, FIE, FO, FUM

FEE, FIE, FO, FUM.
FINGer's GONE and
SO is THUMB.
FEE, FIE, FO, FUM.

LITTLE HANDS

TWO little HANDS go CLAP, clap, CLAP.
TWO little FEET go TAP, tap, TAP.
ONE little BODy goes ROUND and ROUND.
ONE little CHILD sits QUICKly DOWN.

IN THE BIBLE

(Open hands as a book.)

IN the BIble,
IN the BIble,
READ of *JEsus*
IN the BIble.

Help teach some Bible stories with these rhymes. Vary them to fit more lessons. Change "Samuel grew" to "Jesus grew." Instead of "One little sheep" try "One little child went into the church."

SAMUEL GREW

LITtle BAby SAMuel   *(Hold up fist.)*
GREW   *(Raise little finger.)*
and GREW   *(Add fourth finger.)*
and GREW.   *(Add middle finger.)*

JESUS WENT UP

JEsus STANDing   *(Finger on fist hill.)*
ON a HILL

Went UP and UP: *(Raise finger high.)*
He's UP there STILL.

ON THE CROSS

ON the CROSS, ON the CROSS,   *(Form cross with the*
THEY put JEsus ON the CROSS.   *two index fingers.)*

IN the TOMB, IN the TOMB,   *(Close finger inside*
THEY put JEsus IN the TOMB.   *the other hand.)*

UP to HEAVen, UP to HEAVen,   *(Raise both arms.)*
JEsus ROSE and WENT to HEAVen.

ONE LITTLE SHEEP

ONE little SHEEP   *(One finger.)*
Went INto the FOLD.

TWO little SHEEP   *(Two fingers.)*
Went INto the FOLD.

ALL the little SHEEP   *(All fingers.)*
Went INto the FOLD.

80

GOOD KING JOSIAH

GOOD   KING   JoSIah
FIXED the house,   *(Hammering or*
FIXED the house,   *sawing motion.)*
FIXED the house of GOD.

GOOD   PRIEST   HilKIah
FOUND the book,   *(Hands behind back.*
FOUND the book,   *Bring to front and*
FOUND the book of GOD.   *form book.)*

GOOD   KING   JoSIah
READ the book,   *(Stand and hold book.)*
READ the book,
READ the book of GOD.

Make your own words to familiar tunes, and sing just about any Bible truth you want to teach. With "God Made Everything" you can sing about rain, stars, tree, and anything you or the children wish. Also use your children's names.

CHILDREN SHOULD OBEY
(Tune: Mary Had a Little Lamb)

All the children should obey,
Should obey, should obey.
All the children should obey
What their fathers say.

GOD MADE EVERYTHING
(Tune: Farmer in the Dell)

God made the sun.
God made the sun.
God made everything;
God made the sun.

God made Brenda.
God made Brenda.
God made everyone;
God made Brenda.

USEFUL TUNES

Add these useful tunes to your repertoire and use them, also, with your own words. On the first one try "I will be like Jesus," "I will be a helper," and other lines. The second, active, song is very popular—especially the fall. Be a spinning star or a falling leaf or a happy child.

I NEED JESUS

82

I'M A FLYING SPARROW
(Children's Chant)

Sing about the Bible itself. You can use rhythm instruments with this. Supply the melody on the third line yourself with a kazoo (wax paper on a comb). Or just sing la, la, la.

I WILL LOVE THE BIBLE

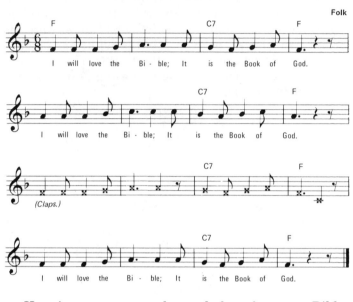

Here is a song to teach vocabulary from any Bible story you happen to be using. Have visuals to show the three objects. Sometimes use children's names; line up three children and sing about them.

ONE IS-A

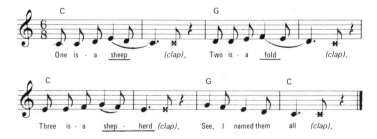

Here are two more songs for using your children's names. Even children who cannot sing the songs will love to hear their names in these. On the first song sing, "Harry wore a bright blue shirt" or "Daniel wore his brand new shoes," or even "Gail brought her favorite doll." On "Jesus Loves the Little Children" stretch out the third line until you include all the names, even if they do not fit the notes.

SALLY WORE A YELLOW DRESS

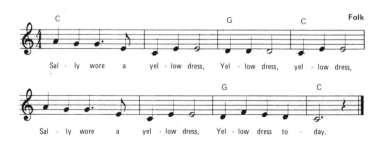

Sal - ly wore a yel - low dress, Yel - low dress, yel - low dress,

Sal - ly wore a yel - low dress, Yel - low dress to - day.

JESUS LOVES THE LITTLE CHILDREN

"Lullaby" and "Soft Things" will help set a quiet mood. Children especially love to say "Sh" at the end of the song, even if they are too little to sing any of the rest of it.

LULLABY

SOFT THINGS

TEACHER: Little fluffy kitten—soft, soft fur—
Stroke it gently, it will say,

CHILDREN: Purr, purr, purr.

TEACHER: Little woolly puppy—soft, not rough—
Stroke it gently, it will say,

CHILDREN: Wuff, wuff, wuff.

TEACHER: Little downy chicken—eyes asleep—
Stroke it gently, it will say,

CHILDREN: Peep, peep, peep.

TEACHER: Little yellow duckling—smooth, smooth back—
Stroke it gently, it will say,

CHILDREN: Quack, quack, quack.

Use this classic. Children everywhere should learn it. They will need it especially when they are grown up.

JESUS LOVES ME

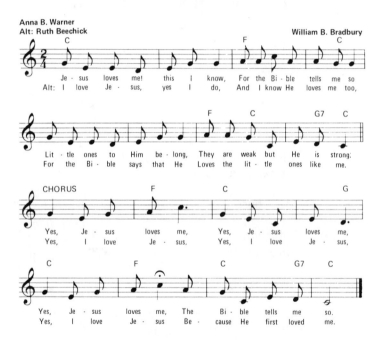

Anna B. Warner
Alt: Ruth Beechick

William B. Bradbury

Je - sus loves me! this I know, For the Bi - ble tells me so
Alt: I love Je - sus, yes I do, And I know He loves me too,

Lit - tle ones to Him be - long, They are weak but He is strong:
For the Bi - ble says that He Loves the lit - tle ones like me.

CHORUS

Yes, Je - sus loves me, Yes, Je - sus loves me,
Yes, I love Je - sus, Yes, I love Je - sus,

Yes, Je - sus loves me, The Bi - ble tells me so.
Yes, I love Je - sus Be - cause He first loved me.

Hand and finger play, as well as larger action will give muscles some of the work they need, and provide helpful interludes between stories.

WHERE IS THUMBKIN?
(Tune: Are You Sleeping?)

1. Where is Thumbkin? *(Hands behind back.)*
   Where is Thumbkin?
   Here I am. *(Bring out one hand, thumb up.)*
   Here I am. *(Other hand.)*
   How are you today? *(Wiggle one thumb.)*
   Very well, I say. *(Wiggle other thumb.)*
   Run away. *(One hand behind back.)*
   Run away. *(Other hand behind back.)*

2. Where is Pointer? *(Use index finger.)*

3. Where is Tall Man? *(Use middle finger.)*

4. Where is Ring Man? *(Use ring finger.)*

5. Where is Little Man? *(Use little finger.)*

6. Where are all the men? *(Use all fingers.)*

Variations: Name the fingers *Mother, Father, Sister, Brother, Baby*. End with the whole family. Try singing about children in the class or about various characters in your Bible stories.

HEAD AND TUMMY

GOD MADE ME—
HEAD and TUMmy,
KNEES and TOES,
LEGS and ARMS
And EARS and NOSE.

*(Touch the body
parts as named.)*

CLAP YOUR HANDS

Clap,   Clap,   Clap your hands.   Clap your hands to - geth - er.

Clap,   Clap,   Clap your hands.   Clap your hands to - geth - er.

Variations: Use rhythm instruments. Sing "Shake, shake,
shake your hands" or "Tap, tap, tap your sticks." Or try "Tap
your feet," "Nod your head," "Stretch your arms," and other
motions for various body parts.

WITH MY HANDS

E.H. (Adapted)

Engelbert Humperdinck (Adapted)

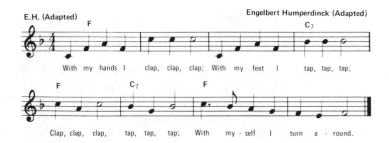

With my hands I   clap, clap, clap; With my feet I   tap, tap, tap;

Clap, clap, clap,   tap, tap, tap;   With   my - self I   turn   a - round.

In each child's life the time will come when counting is more fun than anything. Have these waiting for such a time.

BEEHIVE

HERE is a BEEhive.   *(Closed hand.)*
WHERE are the BEES?
HIDing aWAY where NObody SEES.
They're COMing out NOW;
They're ALL aLIVE.
ONE, two, THREE, four, FIVE.   *(Use fingers.)*

ANTHILL

HERE is an ANThill—   *(Closed hand.)*
NO ants aBOUT.
SO I'll SAY, "Ants, PLEASE come OUT."
They're COMing out NOW;
They're ALL aLIVE.
ONE, two, THREE, four, FIVE.   *(Use fingers.)*

BALLS

A LITtle ball,   *(One hand.)*
A LARGer ball,   *(Two hands.)*
A GREAT big ball I SEE.   *(Both arms.)*

NOW let's count
The BALLS we made—
ONE, two, THREE.   *(Make each ball as counted.)*

READING CHECK

1.　Simple rhymes at nursery-rhyme level have little value in the classroom besides for teaching a few words.

　　　　　　　　　　　　　　　　　　　　T　　F

2.　Songs for young children should be pitched high.

　　　　　　　　　　　　　　　　　　　　T　　F

3.　Only a few preschool children can carry a tune.

　　　　　　　　　　　　　　　　　　　　T　　F

4.　Most preschoolers will not become good group singers during this age.　　　　　　　　　T　　F

5.　Children's spontaneous songs are as important as the teacher's planned songs.　　　　　　T　　F

6.　Children should not have rhythm instruments until they are able to keep the rhythm.　　　　T　　F

Answers: 1—F, 2—F, 3—T, 4—T, 5—T, 6—F

5 How Do You Handle Stories?

Christians are a people of the Book, and teaching the Book naturally involves "book-learning" types of activities. Thus stories have come to be a major part of our teaching in Christian education endeavors with young children. And mastering the use of stories is an important part of a preschool teacher's job.

Preschool-Level Stories

Stories for young preschoolers may not be what you usually think of as stories. They will not depend on causality for their interest. That is, one event does not necessarily happen *because* something else happened. Water is not all over the world because it rained or because the people were wicked. Such linking of events in a causal relationship is beyond the minds of these children. There may be a sequence of events: the rain did come and the boat did float on the water. Samuel heard a voice and it was not Eli, he heard a voice again and it was not Eli, and so forth. Simple sequences are the most advanced kind of story the young children can understand. Many stories will be simply one incident— not a story at all to our adult minds.

Stories also will not depend on a developed concept of

space. For instance, you could not expect the children to understand the whole world and understand it being covered with water; that is too advanced a space concept. Time concepts are beyond preschoolers too. These children who have only lived for two to four years cannot comprehend centuries or millenniums. "Long ago" becomes an absolute in their minds, not a time relative to other times. Long ago can be a story time, almost a place, something concrete and definite. But numbers sometimes are fun: He lived for a hundred years; or you count one, two, three and you just can't count all the stars.

Relationships also are beyond these children's understanding. A little boy may know he is a brother. That is, he may know it is one of the names you can call a boy. But he does not realize it means he is a brother *to* someone. In your stories you may speak of the mother, the grandmother, and so on, but if you use these simply as names for the people, you are more on the level of your children. You can teach that Jesus is God's Son, and the children will learn that as a name for Jesus. It is something He *is,* not a relationship He holds. We must learn not to project our adult, advanced, abstract thinking onto the child. When he uses a word he attaches his limited, concrete meaning to it—if he has any meaning at all—and we can understand him better if we learn to interpret him this way.

This is not to say we avoid all words that imply relationships; that is probably impossible. There is no harm in teaching that Jesus is God's Son. When a child learns this young, he can grow into a better understanding of what it means as his mind grows and develops.

Family relationships are not the only relationships we need to be concerned about in teaching young children. Any relationship meets with the same limitations of understanding—friends and enemies, kings and subjects, and so forth. Relationships should be avoided in stories as much as possible, and when relation words cannot be avoided they should be used in a concrete way. That is the only way children will understand them even if we do misuse them, so we may as well get on their wave length. We will be able to communicate more if we do.

If you have long practice in adapting stories to the child mind you may have good success in telling stories in your own words. But if the stories in your published lessons have been written for reading aloud, it is just as well to read them as they are.

Stories can be accompanied by flannelgraph visuals but this is not the only way to present Bible stories, nor is it necessarily the best. In your teaching program you probably will want to use variety—sometimes puppets, sometimes stand-ups or simple pictures, sometimes picture books, and sometimes flannelgraph or other kinds of visuals.

Picture Books

Of the various kinds of story presentations, the picture book is undoubtedly the classic, all-time favorite of children. A good picture book is a careful blend of pictures and words. There are no solid blocks of print to hold you on a page long after the children want to turn it over. Books for the youngest preschoolers sometimes have only one word per page, as a book which teaches Christmas words—manger, hay, Mary, Baby Jesus and others. More advanced books may have one line or several lines per page. The whole book is a story. A collection of Bible stories with accompanying pictures belongs in the category of illustrated books—not picture books.

A good collection of picture books enhances any preschool classroom. In a Christian setting—in Sunday schools and other church-related programs—they are more important than blocks, crayons, and most other common classroom items. Books for reading to groups need well-defined art that can be distinguished from several feet away. Some picture books may work well on a couch at home, but not with a group of children in a classroom story time.

Public librarians have developed picture book story times over many years and have learned much about conducting them successfully. Sunday school teachers might do well to visit their library story hours and learn from them. One of the major techniques librarians can teach us is how to select a variety of stories for one session. There is no need, and apparently no advantage, to restrict children to only one story. A picture book session consists of several stories interspersed with action rhymes or other kinds of movement, an occasional song, and a little conversation. It can last for twenty-five minutes or more. After the stories are read, the children usually spend a few more moments looking at books themselves. Here are some more techniques that will help you run a successful picture book session.

Hold a book so the children can see the pictures and so you can turn pages without obscuring the view. To do this you grip the book firmly with one hand at either top or bottom and hold it in front of you or out at one side. The free hand turns pages from either top or bottom. Learn to do all this without giving the children a wobbly view of the story. Never turn the book toward you for reading and then toward the children for viewing. Such a chopped-up story is extremely distracting. The book should be very nearly at eye level, or if there is more than one row of children it should be slightly above the heads of the children in the front row.

Learn to enhance the story with your voice and expression. The most common fault of beginners is reading too fast. Watch this. The listeners need more time to absorb the story than does the reader, so read slowly enough for the children to catch each word. Use expression as it comes naturally; you do not need to be overly dramatic. Watch that your voice does not unintentionally rise in pitch; a low-pitched voice tends to calm the children. Starting out in a soft, low tone helps attract their attention.

The children should be seated in a shallow semicircle. If they are using chairs, space these far enough apart to allow elbow room. If they are sitting on the floor, teach them to test out their elbowroom and move if necessary. Or you move them, if they don't understand what to do. If there are distractions—traffic or bright sunlight, or other classes in view—be sure to arrange things so the children's backs are toward the distraction and you are the one facing it.

Do not expect complete silence or complete absence of wiggling. Wiggling does not necessarily indicate lack of attention. Ignore minor disturbances, if possible, and keep the story going. Sometimes just saying a child's name is enough to quiet a growing disturbance: "And, Valerie, that's just what Noah did." If a child asks to go to the bathroom, you might say, "Wait just a moment; we'll have time for that later." Then he may forget it for several moments, until your fast-moving story session is over. In any interruption you cannot ignore, try as much as possible not to make a "thing" of it. Don't let it become a full-blown disciplinary situation. Respond as briefly as you can and continue with your story session. Remember that your young children are rather new to such group listening experiences. Some may be entirely new. You are the one teaching them how to manage, and it takes time.

If interest lags during a story, you can skip parts, bring it to a quick close, and introduce an active interlude—an action song or rhyme, or a play-the-story scene. The children can stretch up high and rain down rain with their fingers all the way to the floor, then repeat and rain some more rain. Many simple actions taken from your stories will provide good exercise.

Some books call for the children to participate in the story. A simple word book that names one object or person per page can be read by most children after they have heard it a few times. Books with patterned repetition invite the children to complete the patterns. Books with questions invite the children to give the answers. Be alert to words the children will be able to anticipate and say with you, and pause to give them time to do this. The first time these books are introduced they should be read twice or even more times so the children can have opportunity to participate. In subsequent story sessions when the books are reviewed, it is not always necessary to repeat them twice; you should be guided by the children's interest and their memory of each book.

After a story session sometimes you can let each child take a book to look at—those you have just read and others too. You will need more books than children. When a child finishes looking at a book he trades it for another. Either you hand him the trade, or he chooses it from a table, and he returns his other book. Some children will spend a long time looking at one book and trying to read it; others will leaf quickly through the pages and trade off a number of books during this time. It is the children's private time to use books, each in his own way.

In a well-run, happy story time, much learning happens. You will see a tiny bit of it—the tip of the potato plant peeking above the ground. After a series of sessions you will see the sprout growing, but much of the learning—like the potatoes—is hidden from your view. Parts of it surface from time to time in the responses of the children, and these parts are indications to you of inner growth and learning.

Children can play with blocks at home or day school, they can color any time, they have their individual learning experiences—examining flowers and so forth—

all week long. When you have your children for an hour or so at church, you can contribute a good group learning experience—with books—for at least part of the hour.

Flannelgraph

Flannelgraph visuals have long been popular with children's Bible teachers. Sometimes they have been overrated, and teachers expect a kind of magic from them that they cannot deliver. Children do not, for instance, remember any given percentage of information just because they have seen it on a board. And children will not understand difficult concepts just because they have been visualized with flannelgraph figures. All the limitations of the child mind are there no matter what format is used for presenting a story.

Space concepts, for instance, are not clarified by space on a flannelboard. If Jonah runs away from Nineveh, or people travel across a desert, or water covers the earth, children cannot translate the flannelboard view into a mental picture of the whole earth, or a long, hot desert journey, or the complicated geography of the Jonah story. For the children, the story takes place on the board. It is here and now.

To communicate well, you do not attempt to raise the children to your kind of understanding, but you attempt to move yourself into their kind of thinking. This is not as difficult as it may sound. Many teachers were doing this instinctively long before Piaget came on the scene and explained to us the child view of time, space, causality, concreteness and so forth. None of these things are really new to experienced children's workers; what is new in our Piaget generation is the systematized theory of the development of the mind that Piaget has formulated, and the scientific rigor with which these things are now being measured and studied. But you always knew that young children could not understand abstractions, didn't you? You didn't need science to tell you that. As you work with children you can grow in your understanding of them and your ability to communicate on their level.

Flannelgraph stories can have some of the features that are in good picture books—naming, sequence, repetition, patterned form. Several of these features combine in this example of a flannelgraph presentation at nursery-rhyme level.

This is the sheepfold.   *(Place sheepfold on board.)*

This is the sheep   *(Place sheep in fold.)*
that lives in the sheepfold.

This is the grass   *(Add grass.)*
that feeds the sheep
that lives in the sheepfold.

This is the pasture   *(Add pasture.)*
that grows the grass
that feeds the sheep
that lives in the sheepfold.

That is the shepherd   *(Add shepherd.)*
that finds the pasture
that grows the grass
that feeds the sheep
that lives in the sheepfold.

(From Accent On Life Bible Curriculum. Used by permission)

Except for the sheep being placed in the fold, all the pieces are arranged in a row. The storyteller points back across the row each time, and the children name each picture, and participate in the story. Children can play games with the pieces: "Which one is missing?" or "Who can give me the one that finds the grass?" They also can sing about the pictures. (See the song, "One Is-a" in Chapter 4.)

This is flannelgraph being used in the here and now. There is no attempt to transport children to long-ago and far-away; it all happens on the board. The system of simply arranging things in a row is a useful one. It helps children grasp story sequence. Noah built a boat, the animals and family went in, water came, and afterward the rainbow came. The tiny mustard seed grew to a little plant and then to a big plant. In stories like these the visual pieces are simply placed across the board in story order (always from left to right). Children can retell the story by telling about each piece, they can play games of putting them in order, and in these processes they are not only learning the immediate story, but are developing an important basic understanding called story sequence.

In some stories it is appropriate to move visual pieces. Esther can move from her house over to Uncle's house to live. But if you are trying to omit space and relational concepts from your stories, you will find these occasions rare.

Items can be counted, they can be removed as in the lost sheep, they can be arranged in formations such as inside the fold or outside the fold, they can be built up as in repairing the temple or building Noah's ark. In all these maneuvers the important basic principle to remember is that it happens here and now for the children. It is visible, concrete, and there on the story-board.

This does not mean you will never use "space" words or "time" words. There are occasions when these words are unavoidable. You may want to begin a story with, "This is Jesus. One day long, long ago . . ." But if you are in tune with the children's minds you will not expect such words to produce the same result they do in your own mind. The children will not transport themselves back 2000 years in history to the time of Jesus, but they may—after the good story experiences you provide—learn to transport themselves to a story time. This is a beautiful time and place all wrapped into one, that happens only in childhood, and afterward is lost forever, except to a few fortunate writers and storytellers who can occasionally return to visit it.

When using flannelgraph there are the practical matters of furniture and class arrangement to consider. All the suggestions given in the picture book section also apply here. In addition, you have the flannelboard itself—and that does need some thought. Too often classrooms are provided with high, wobbly easels whose picture area slants toward the ceiling, and the children are provided with low chairs or carpet squares from which they crane their necks to see. The remedy for this is obvious; you need to obtain a low easel and sit, rather than stand, as you use it. Or use no easel at all, but a lap board. With one of these, you hold the board on your lap with one hand and place figures with the other. You look down from the top of the board, but are careful not to slant it more than what is needed to hold the figures. Your waiting figures can be on your knees or on a chair beside you.

Puppets

Puppets have become very popular, and numerous books on their use are available. With young preschoolers, puppetry does not need to be a complicated matter with theaters, stage settings and elaborate puppets. Paper bag puppets, stick puppets, finger puppets, and other simple kinds being used with the puppeteer in full view work just fine. The children will often wear the hand or finger puppets themselves, and learn to say some of the story lines for the puppet.

Puppets add variety; they can occasionally be used as story visuals, as well as with finger plays and action

songs. But teachers with a deep interest in puppetry really should take their talents to an older department in the church. The young children of the early preschool ages are still busy learning about themselves and about others. They are new at human interpersonal relationships, and they need to learn their important life lessons from real humans in real relationships. A stage or box (even a "live" TV kind) with puppets and cartoon characters is a poor substitute for real people in a child's life.

A teacher in training remarked, "You have to be careful what the puppets say because the children are really going to remember it." This is utter nonsense. The implication here is that there is something magic— something superhuman—about puppets that can teach children better than real, live humans can. A child does not learn important lessons in living better from a puppet than from another human, but he will enjoy having his teachers use puppets.

With a scaled-down, common-sense view of puppets you may safely introduce them into your classroom. Children do love them—particularly the everyday kind of characters that are close to children's lives and understandable to them. Some published lessons use little boy and girl puppets, much like the preschool children themselves. In a church that began using such puppets parents asked the teacher who these new children were. "All I hear after Sunday school nowadays is talk about the new pupils in your class." The teacher smiled and replied that the two children named were the new puppets.

Animal puppets are popular with young children, too. This is the age when talking animals appeal the most. Even inanimate objects—nature items, for instance—can be worn as puppets. Do not keep the puppets for yourself or for "performers" but encourage the children to use them. Children can use the puppets and say lines from the stories and rhymes.

Other Visuals

Published lessons come with a variety of story visuals—sometimes stand-up characters to move on a table, or pocket characters to move in a pocket storyboard. To get maximum benefit from these, you should allow the children to use them just as you do with flannelgraph figures or puppets. If interlocking tabs are flimsy and pieces fall apart when handled, try taping things together, mounting on cardboard, and other procedures you can invent to make them more childproof.

Flat pictures are an old and still popular kind of visual. They have the disadvantage that they cannot be manipulated as flannelgraph or stand-ups or others. But they have advantages too. They can show background and more complete scenes. Items stay in the same, recognizable position, as the words in a favorite story or rhyme. And teachers like the fact that they can be placed on a wall where children see them again and again and learn to tell about the stories that go with them. Pictures have other uses besides as story visuals. Some of these were given in Chapter 2.

Sometimes use the children and yourself as living visuals. Have a boy come to the front and pretend to be sick and you be the father who goes to get Jesus. You tell the story as the action goes along, and the children in their seats watch.

Closely related to living visuals, is the well-known activity of playing the story. This of course is visual, but also is kinesthetic, or motion, learning. In this activity all the children play the major part, instead of just one or two doing it for the others to watch. You need to build up the momentum for this and keep it going by a steady stream of talking. Tell the children, "We're Joseph. We're going out to look for the brothers. Let's walk this way. We'll walk and walk, and climb up this hill. Now look over the hill. Do you see the brothers? No, they're not there. Let's go over the next hill." In this manner you lead the children through the story. After playing the story it is often a good idea to sit down and read the picture book, or tell the original story once again. The children will understand it better the second time, after having gone through the motions themselves.

Sound Stories

Some stories lend themselves to a sound effects version, and these can be just as informal as playing the story, with you making up the details as you go along. For instance, to do the same story of Joseph described above, you could have the children practice making walking sounds by slapping their hands on their laps. (*Patter, patter, patter, pat.*) Then begin to tell the story, pausing as needed for the walking sounds. If you do the pattering too, the children have no problem knowing when to help. It might go like this. "Joseph started out to look for his brothers." *(Patter, patter, patter, pat.)* "He went over the first mountain." *(Patter, patter, patter, pat.)* "He went over the second mountain." *(Patter, patter, patter, pat.)* "He began to get tired and went very slowly." *(Pat-ter . . . pat-ter . . . pat.)* "But he kept going anyway." *(Patter, patter, patter, pat.)* Continue in this manner until Joseph finds his brothers.

If your children like these and can follow pretty well you could try some in which they have more than one sound. For the Noah story you could have them try to make the sound of raindrops by tapping with fingers on the chairs or the floor. Make the sound of wind by whooshing air through your teeth. Make sounds of various animals which were in the boat: cats, dogs, chickens, lions, and others. The sound of Noah pounding boards can be made by stomping feet. When the children have practiced each of the sounds it would be fun to go through each of them again; the children will enjoy it more when they know better what to do. Then do a story similar to this.

Noah built a great big boat. *(Pound feet.)*

Noah brought to the boat some cats *(meow)*, some dogs *(bow wow)*, some chickens *(cluck, cluck)*, some lions *(roar)*. *(Name as many animals as you wish.)*

Then the rain began to fall. *(Tap fingers.)*

And Noah had a boat ride. A long, long boat ride.

After a time the wind began to blow. *(Whoosh.)* It blew and blew and blew. *(Whoosh.)*

Then the water all went away. And Noah came out of the boat. And out came the cats *(meow)*, the dogs *(bow wow)*, the chickens *(cluck, cluck)*, the lions *(roar)*. *(Name all the animals you named the first time.)*

And Noah's boat ride was all done.

(From Accent On Life Bible Curriculum. Used by permission.)

You could write out some of your sound stories and keep them on cards, along with action rhymes, to use over and over again with the same wording each time. Here is an example from I Samuel 9.

> Saul goes over the mountain.
> > *(Patter, patter, patter, pat.)*
> He goes through the land.
> > *(Patter, patter, patter, pat.)*
> He goes through the next land.
> > *(Patter, patter, patter, pat.)*
> He goes to the man.
> > *(Patter, patter, patter, pat.)*
> He goes home again.
> > *(Patter, patter, patter, pat.)*
> The donkeys are found.

(From Accent On Life Bible Curriculum. Used by permission.)

READING CHECK

1. Understanding of causal relationship is within the children's cognitive abilities.   T   F
2. Grasping a sequence of events is within the children's cognitive abilities.   T   F
3. A teacher should never read stories to children, but should tell them in her own words.   T   F
4. A teacher should not use a story the children have had before, lest it bore them.   T   F
5. A teacher should not read several stories in one sitting lest it confuse the children.   T   F
6. Flannelgraph is not necessarily the best kind of visual.   T   F
7. Children remember something better if they hear a puppet say it.   T   F
8. Sound stories are not as good as flannelgraph stories because they have no visuals.   T   F

Answers: 1—F, 2—T, 3—F, 4—F, 5—F, 6—T, 7—F, 8—F

6 What about Games and Movement?

Do these children really play games? These youngest of children, just out of toddlerhood? We think of the egocentric character of the child mind—how he cannot understand an opponent to compete with him, or understand a teammate to cooperate with him. We think of how he cannot understand relationships, so necessary for appreciating a score or goal of a game.

When we consider what these children are like, we find that they are largely in a pre-game stage. As with all "stages" we use to describe children's development, this does not have hard and fast boundary lines. Games come in all levels of complexity and children come with varying levels of development too. But generally speaking, we can call this the pre-game level.

So, do we use games for these children? Yes. What we do is design pre-games. Pre-games do not depend on competition, scoring or winning for their interest. Pre-games do not depend on cooperation. In most of these games each child can do his own thing regardless of what the others are doing. As in parallel play, children can act together but not together, act alongside each other but separately. In some few games, such as "One Little, Two Little," there seems to be a measure of cooperation, but it is cooperation in form, not intent. It is an outer look of cooperation, not the inner reality, but as such it is a step toward more game-like cooperation. All pre-games are steps toward the classical games of older childhood. They are ways to help children learn and develop. So we make a place for them in our preschool classrooms.

Games with Cards and Visuals

One of the most flexible teaching devices you can have is a set of cards pertaining to whatever topic you wish to teach. Often you will be able to make such a set yourself if the lessons you are using do not provide one. An easy-to-make set could have pictures of things God made. Either collect pictures to paste on your cards, or draw simple pictures of things God made—flower, tree, bird, sun, moon, stars, and other objects. Here are some games you can play with this set of cards.

Naming. This is a good game to start with. It helps the children become familiar with the cards before they graduate to more advanced games with them. Simply hold up a card and let the children name it. Give the card to a child who named it, and show the next one. When all the cards have been given out, collect them and repeat.

Tell Me. Hold the cards so the children cannot see the pictures. Ask the children to tell you a card you hold. When any child names an item, hand him the card he names. When all the cards have been given out, collect and repeat. This game gives the children practice in forming mental images, as they must "image" a picture which is not in view.

Bring Me. Set all the cards face up on the floor or somewhere in full view of the children and ask questions like these. "Who can bring me the one birds build nests in?" Who can bring me the one that shines in the daytime?" When all the cards have been collected, lay them down again and ask new questions to repeat the game. For instance, on the tree you might ask, "Who can bring me the one that has leaves?" If there is too much confusion and fighting over the cards when you use the word *who*, try "Sally, bring me the one that . . . " For very young children, you can simplify this by asking for the card only by name. "Sally, bring me the tree." This game helps build meaning behind the word and picture symbols.

Choose One. Scramble the cards and place them face down where all the children can see. Let a volunteer pick up a card, name it, and hand it to you. When all the cards are collected, scramble again and repeat.

Which One Is Missing? Begin this game with only three of the cards. Let everyone see the three and practice naming them. Then scramble the cards and lay them face down. Remove one card. Let a child turn over the other two. All the children look at them and try to tell you which card is missing. Repeat several times. Make the game more difficult by using four or more cards.

One Is-a. Let a child choose any three of the cards and place them in a row on the floor or on your easel ledge. All sing the song "One Is-a" (See Chapter 4), naming the three items in order. Use either claps or some kind of rhythm instrument. Shakers are especially good; on the last note shake as hard as you can for as long as you want. Or do the same with clapping. Let another child choose three pictures and put them in his own order. Sing again.

Guess. Some sets of cards will lend themselves to actions—a set of helping cards, for instance. With these you can look at a card and then pantomime the action. Let the children guess. Sometimes certain of your children may be able to act out the cards for others to guess.

Here are some other ideas for card sets.

1. *Christmas words:* manger, hay, Baby Jesus, Mary, shepherds.

2. *Easter words:* cross, tomb, angel, Peter or others who appear in the stories you use.
3. *Bible animals:* sheep, camel, donkey, goat.
4. *Noah's animals:* elephant, frog, giraffe, bear, etc.
5. *Helping cards:* spoons (to put in drawer or set the table with), bed (to make), trike (to put away), broom, rake, door (to close without slamming).
6. *Obeying cards:* similar to above, showing things a child will do when a parent asks him to.
7. *Family cards:* mother, father, baby, brother, sister, grandma.
8. *Praying cards:* showing when you can talk to God—in bed, at the table, at play, in Sunday school class, in the car.
9. *Colors God made:* blue, red, green, yellow, brown, black.
10. *Number cards:* one sheep, two sheep, three sheep, four sheep. Or one flower, etc.

Matching games take a somewhat different set of cards. They must come in pairs—shoe and foot, mitten and hand, cap and head, or bird and nest, bee and hive, rabbit and hole. One element of each pair could be put onto a larger game board. This makes matching easier for the younger children; they find a card to match each item on the board and set each in its place.

Sorting games are another variation. The board must have two parts—day and night, for instance, or Mommy and Daddy. Cards with things we do in the daytime go on the day side, or cards showing daddies doing things go on the Daddy side.

When introducing matching games or sorting games do them first with the whole group. Set the board where all can see it. Hold up one card and ask who knows where it belongs. Let a volunteer put the card in place. Continue until all cards are matched or sorted. By this group procedure many children will learn how to do the games.

They can later play these games individually at an activity table or other area where you keep such items as games and puzzles.

Some of the games described above can also be used with visual pieces—flannelgraph figures, standup figures, or any other kind. With three or more pieces you could use the games, "Naming," "Tell Me," "Bring Me," "Which One Is Missing?" and the song, "One Is-a."

Flannelgraph figures sometimes lend themselves to other types of games. If your story is about Esther moving from her house to Uncle's house to live you can later play "Where Is Esther?" Hide Esther behind a house and let the children guess and lift the houses to find her. Make extra houses from brightly colored felt for this game. If your story is about finding the lost Book of God or the lost sheep you could make similar games. Hide the lost items behind pieces of felt. Let the children guess and look.

Games of "Arranging" can be played with several of any one item—for instance, several houses. Make big and little houses, and red and blue houses. A simple version of the game is to set the houses down and give directions for a child to place them on the board. "Put the big house up high and two little houses down low." "Put the blue houses on this side and the red house on that side." "Line up all the houses in a row." "Put up the house you like best." For the youngest children, give only single directions. More mature children can handle double directions.

A more advanced version of Arranging is to let a child arrange the houses and then describe what he has done. You may have to ask questions to help him talk about his arranging. Other felt pieces which can be used in games of Arranging are sheep or other animals, children, nature items.

Hiding games are fun away from the flannelboard as well as on. Hide paper sheep around the room—enough for all the children to find some. Or hide paper "books" or Joseph's brothers. Try a more difficult version of Hiding. Have the children look for paper faces and leave all the sad faces where they are but pick up the happy faces to keep.

Singing Games

"The Mulberry Bush" is a useful tune; use it to teach various actions from your Bible lessons, or use it for exercise.

> This is the way we go to church,
> Go to church, go to church,
> This is the way we go to church
> So early in the morning.

Sing "This is the way we read our Bibles" or "talk to God" or "carry water" or "watch our sheep." Or sing, "This is the way we touch our toes," or "jump up high." Pantomime the actions or do the exercises as you sing. Young children, remember, do not easily do two things at once so they may leave most of the singing to you. There is no need to make a circle formation; each child can stand wherever he is and participate. Sometimes let the children help think of actions to sing about.

"Did You Ever See a Lassie" will give children even more opportunity to try to think of actions. Bring Lori to the front of the class, or to the center of the circle if your children can deal with circle formations.

ALL: Did you ever see our Lori,
         Our Lori, our Lori,
         Did you ever see our Lori
         Go this way and that?

TEACHER: Do something.

LORI: Touches toes, claps hands, hops around, or
         other action. *(Whisper an idea in her ear if she
         needs one.)*

ALL: *(Imitating Lori's actions.)*
         Go this way and that way,
         Go this way and that way,
         Did you ever see our Lori
         Go this way and that?

Choose a new lassie or laddie and repeat. To use a child's own name and sing about him, giving him attention in this way, will help him develop his concept of self and of self in relation to the class. Children need many of these kinds of experiences.

"Merrily We Roll Along" is another easy tune to exercise with. You or the children think of something to do and then sing and do it. After the stanza think of the next thing to do. Each exercise ends either with "Let your hands go clap," or "Let your feet go stamp." Here are some examples.

1. Touch your toes and then your knees,
   Touch your toes and then your knees,
   Touch your toes and then your knees,
   And let your hands go clap.

2. Hug yourself and turn around,
   Hug yourself and turn around,
   Hug yourself and turn around,
   And let your feet go stamp.

3. Touch the floor and stand up tall.

4. Lift your foot and kick the ball.

5. Stand on tiptoe, turn around.

6. Point your toe and take a bow.

7. Bend your body up and down.

"Row, Row, Row Your Boat" can turn your children into birds or butterflies. Let them "fly" anywhere they like, as you sing.

> Fly, fly, fly away,
> Fly away up high.
> Fly, fly, fly away,
> Fly away up high.

For older children who are mature enough for a game with an "ending," try this version and have them fly away from you and back to you as the song says.

> Fly, fly, fly away,
> Fly, away from me.
> Fly, fly, fly away,
> And quick fly back to me.

Sing "I Was Glad." Then make a game version of it by using each child's name. Take a child by the hand, lead him around the room and back to his seat "in church."

I WAS GLAD

Psalm 122:1

I was glad, I was glad when they said to me,
Alt: Johnny's glad, Johnny's glad when they say to him,

"Let us go, let us go to the house of the Lord."

(Adapted from Accent On Life Bible Curriculum. Used with permission.)

Classic Games, Simplified

Simon Says. In the classic Simon Says the leader gives commands and the followers are to carry them out only when they are preceded by the phrase, "Simon says." For little children you can leave out the choice of whether or not to follow the commands and simply expect the children to do them all. Say "Mother says Touch the floor," "Mother says Jump," "Father says Turn around," "Father says Reach up high" and so forth. Use the game to help teach the idea of obedience. Also use it to help work the wiggles out; make it as active as your children require. After playing the game, sometimes you can talk about things the children's parents ask them to do at home. Talk about obeying.

Which Hand? This is one of the earliest games that children can learn to do alone, without a teacher. Use a piece of crayon or any small object. "It" puts his hands behind him and closes his fists, one of them with the crayon in it. Then he presents both clenched fists to a guesser, who taps one. If the guesser is correct he takes the crayon and becomes It. If he is not correct, It repeats the procedure again. When playing in a group, choose a new guesser each time.

Sometimes you can relate this game to your lesson by using different objects to hide in the fists. For instance, get a small pebble, add two eyes with felt pen, and it becomes a sheep or fish. Use an acorn or other seed when learning that God makes things grow. With a little imagination you can think of other lesson-related ideas when you need them.

Follow the Leader. There is an endless variety of ways to use this. "Now we will fly like birds." Flap arms, standing in place or moving about the room. "Now we will hop like frogs." "Now we will touch the wall over there." The difference between the preschool version and the older child's version of this game is that you omit any need for formation. The children do not follow you in a line and go where you go, changing actions when you change actions. Instead, there is free formation, and one action announced at a time.

Pretend

Activities in this category are very informal, and you can often make them up on the spot when movement is needed. Get your ideas from almost any Bible story. Does Samuel help in the temple? You and the children together can pretend to be Samuel. Dust the table, sweep the floor, polish the candlestick, and open the big doors for all the people to come in. Does Noah build a boat? Pretend to carry heavy boards, lift them in place, and hammer in the nails. Later smear pitch into all the cracks. Did Jesus heal the little girl? The children can pretend to get sicker and sicker until their life is going away. You be the father to go get Jesus. When you come back with Jesus He says, "Get up, little girl." All the children get up from bed and eat.

Are you learning about sheep? Be sheep and leave the fold in the morning. Eat grass, drink water, take a nap. Go home to the fold again at night. What does a camel do? Kneel down and let someone put a load on your back. Whine and groan because you don't like it. Slowly stand up. Kick out your foot because you are angry. Carry your heavy load a long way. Kneel and let someone take it off again.

Be animals coming to the ark. Be growing trees that God made. Be yourself. Squat down to show how little you were when you were a baby. Slowly grow up until you get as big as you are now. Do it again; grow very slowly.

Sometimes you can translate a fingerplay into a larger movement activity. Here is an example using the fingerplay, "One Little Sheep."

> ONE little SHEEP
> Went INto the FOLD.
>
> TWO little SHEEP
> Went INto the FOLD.
>
> ALL the little SHEEP
> Went INto the FOLD.

On the first verse tap a child on the head and he goes to the fold—a corner of the room, or other designated spot. On the second verse tap another child on the head. He goes into the fold, too. On the third verse all the children leave their seats and crowd into the fold. This last part is such fun that you will have to repeat this several times. Of course, some children will stay in their seats and watch the proceedings. That is normal; let them watch.

Do not force participation in any of your activities.

If your children can handle circle formations, you might let the circle itself be the fold. One child goes to the center, a second child goes, and then all the children crowd in together.

Informal movement activities are easy for a teacher to handle. They require no advance preparations. They provide large muscle movement and kinesthetic learning, as well as helping children form mental images of the actions. There often is vocabulary learning associated with these activities too.

These activities are a useful part of your teaching repertoire. You can include one or more of them in every class session.

READING CHECK

1. Preschool children are likely to have difficulty singing and playing at the same time in a game. T F

2. A teacher should insist that all children take part in games. T F

3. Games promote many kinds of learning. T F

4. About the only use for games is to provide needed movement. T F

5. Which of these elements are most characteristic of the pre-games described in this chapter?

   a. competition
   b. cooperation
   c. scoring system or goal
   d. problem-solving tasks
   e. winning and losing
   f. parallel action
   g. teacher-led
   h. sequence with an ending

Answers: 1—T, 2—F, 3—T, 4—F, 5—d (See, for example, the card games.), f ("Simon Says" is a perfect example, as are practically all singing games and pretend games; problem-solving card games are also largely parallel when used in small groups, and turns are not a factor.), g (Practically all games; some few, as "Which Hand" can eventually be done without a teacher.), h (Hiding games, "Fly Away from Me," and "One Little Sheep" are good examples of games with endings.)

7 Procedures, Equipment, Environment

Helping Children Begin

Some children who come to you may have been attending the church crib room and toddler room since they were born. They may be well adjusted to this separation from parents so that moving into preschool class is no problem at all. But other children may have separation problems as they begin coming to your class.

There are various ways to try handling this. Sometimes the mother will know better than you what should be done. For instance, a mother may know whether she can tell her child goodbye and then leave even if tears start. This procedure works with many children, as once the mother is gone and the child is led to an interesting activity he stops his crying. Other times it may be necessary for a mother to sit in the room for a time or two until her child is secure enough to venture into activities on his own.

One thing you should never do is let the parent sneak away. A child needs to learn to trust early in life, and it is important that he be able to trust his parents and teachers. It is better to have a firm goodbye and a reassuring, "I'll be back soon," and some tears, than to let the parent slip out when the child's back is turned.

Children have varying reactions to new experiences. Some may show their fear and anger by crying, running away, or saying "Go away." In these cases you should try to let the child know you understand how he feels. Some children respond to fear by withdrawal. They may follow directions and do what they are supposed to do, but it is from fear of doing otherwise. There is no spontaneity or reaction. If you recognize a child in this plight you should, again, try to let him know you understand—not with a long "talking to" but with brief, simple remarks.

Some children act silly when they are afraid they have been forgotten or ignored. Give these children lots of attention so they will not need to act silly. Keep treating this symptom with attention, and the need for treatment will gradually lessen. Some children become bullies, trying to prove they are big and strong, and not afraid. Give these children plenty of assurance about themselves, and their surroundings, their parents' returning, and so forth. Treat the fear and not the bullyism. Treat the cause and let the symptom die of uselessness.

This does not mean you should give attention right at the moment a child acts up, since a good technique for classroom control is to ignore misbehavior when you can and turn your attention to children who are behaving properly. But it does mean you should become aware of which children need special attention and assurance from you, and plan to help these children as much as you can. Show all children understanding as much as you can, and love them. As you help children overcome fear and accept new experiences you are helping them toward an all-important basic trust, and toward an improved ability to learn.

Schedules
Each situation requires its own tailor-made schedule. A one-hour Sunday school time requires one kind of schedule and a two- or three-hour extended morning session, requires another kind. The longer

session requires also a consideration of whether it is mostly the same children all morning long, or whether there is a large turnover for the second half, as sometimes happens in churches on a system of double services. In this situation you may want to give the "second service" children as much teaching as the first ones receive. The amount of space, available outdoor area, equipment—all these and more need to be considered.

In the longer sessions there is usually a change of staff with one teacher or group responsible for Sunday school time and another responsible for church time. In these cases it is tempting and convenient for each group to operate quite independently of the other group, but it would be better if they could cooperate at least on working out a total morning schedule so the children have a good mix of active and quiet time, and structured and free time. The children's toileting, rest time and snack time need to be planned from the perspective of the total morning.

In setting up a Sunday morning schedule you need to remember the special purposes of church education. You are not in business to duplicate what is done in secular preschools and day-care centers. Just because something is "educational" or good for the children's development does not necessarily mean it should be included in church programs. What you should strive to do is use time in the best way you can to further your Christian education goals.

If you are planning for a one-hour Sunday school time, it is best to begin with the schedule suggested in the lesson material you are using. With that as a starting point you can make adjustments as needed to fit your situation. In a one-hour schedule it is not necessary to include all the components of a normal preschool morning. For instance, active free play is not necessarily needed. And if your space as well as your time is limited you will not want to include it in your schedule. Quiet free play may be needed if, for instance, the activities you plan do not "catch on" and hold attention as long as you would like. Or if you want opportunity to work with one or two children at a time in a particular activity, you could do this while the others play. Or if you want to use play time to get to know the children better, or help them adjust to the classroom, or learn to do things with friends. There are good uses for play time and children need it often during their week, but they do not necessarily need it during their one hour of Sunday school time.

Here is a schedule some teachers follow which does not make use of free play time. The minutes here are to give a general idea of the time, but actually the periods are flexible and would not be quite the same from Sunday to Sunday.

10 minutes   Arrival time. Greeting children, listening to them. Earlier arrivers may work puzzles, help the teacher with preparations and so forth.

30 minutes   Group learning time. Stories, songs, action rhymes, games, play-the-story, conversation and other planned learning experiences.

15 minutes   Handwork time. Planned handwork. Often a take-home, lesson-related sheet. Clay or other materials available for those who finish quickly.

5 minutes   Closing time. Gather papers and belongings. Talk about what we did today and what we learned.

A schedule that lasts more than two hours needs to provide for these: (1) active play, outdoors if possible, (2) quiet play, (3) rest, (4) toileting and washing, (5) nourishment. If your program is two and one-half hours, as many are now, and if you add transportation time both coming and going, this is quite a long time for the child, and you can see the necessity for the items listed above. Some schools provide for toileting as soon as the child arrives, including this along with other arrival time matters. Here is a schedule that can be used for a two and one-half hour session.

10 minutes	Arrival time. Greeting children, listening to them. Simple activities for the earliest children.
30 minutes	Group learning. Stories, songs, action rhymes, games, play-the-story, conversation and other planned learning experiences.
30 minutes	Handwork. Planned handwork with take-home sheet followed by free choice handwork, including crayons, paints, clay, sorting, stringing, puzzles and other table activities. Clean up.
Transition	Children who leave after Sunday school are leaving one by one as parents call for them during the latter part of the handwork time. Church workers are replacing Sunday school workers during that period and the following one. Sunday school workers stay until their replacements arrive.

20 minutes Active play. Outdoors if possible. Or use large indoor equipment—climbing, riding wheel toys, sliding, etc. If limited space, then use teacher-directed active games.

10 minutes Toileting, washing. Some children can begin preparing table for snack.

10 minutes Snack. Quiet, leisurely time to enjoy snack and enjoy one another. Children can pour own juice, set napkins, serve snack, pray. Teacher joins, and converses with children.

10 minutes Rest. Lie on mats or towels. Play quiet music, or sing to the children.

20 minutes Group learning. Stories, songs, games, and so forth. Examine and talk about a flower or something God made. Learn from pictures, books, objects.

10 minutes Quiet play. Say goodbye to children one at a time as parents call for them.

Space and Equipment

Recommendations for the amount of indoor space range from around 35 square feet to 60 square feet per child. Taking the higher figure, this translates into a room of 20 x 30 for a class of ten children. This kind of space is far from what most churches have today. The lower recommendation translates into a room of about 20 x 17 for ten children. This comes closer to what some churches provide, but a good many teachers at the present time get along with much less than that.

It should be pointed out that churches usually are not offering as full a program as the weekday preschools, and their needs are different. Certainly a church which has the children sit with parents during the worship service and follows only the one-hour Sunday school schedule given above, can get along with much less space than these recommendations. A church with a full morning schedule can also get along with less space by planning carefully to contain the children's more active and more space-taking activities, or making more use of outdoor space. In a once-a-week program this is not the serious problem it would be in a daily program.

A good study is needed of the church preschool situation, to come up with general space recommendations for church planners. Until that is done a sensible goal for most churches is to try to come closer to the minimum day school recommendations. At least there should be more room per child for the preschool and kindergarten departments than for any of the older departments.

Preschool rooms should be at ground level with outdoor play area opening directly off the indoor area. Washrooms and toilet also should open directly from the main classroom. These arrangements greatly simplify the supervision of children, and make it easier to keep the program flexible enough to meet the children's needs. Large, low windows are good, especially if there is any sort of view. If there are just to be walkways full of people, it may be better to keep the windows high, but still let in plenty of light.

Outside doors should have childproof latches. Walls need plenty of space for pinning or taping up the children's work—at the low level of the children's eyes, not the parents' and teachers'. Floors are important, since children spend much time there. No bare concrete or cold drafts should be tolerated. Warm, easily cleaned floors are needed. Rugs or carpet in a part of the room is nice. Chairs, tables, toilets, washbasins, drinking fountains all should be child height. Sturdy steps to the fountains and basins can help in an already built church that was poorly planned in this respect.

Storage space should be ample, and of all kinds—high for the teacher, low for the children, open shelves, and closed doors. The wide, open shelves are the kind most frequently missing in churches. There may be a feeling that for neatness' sake or to keep things safe from older children and other groups who use the room it is necessary to keep everything put behind closed doors. But there are some clever ways to get around these problems. One solution is rolling cabinets which can be turned open side out during preschool classes and then turned to face the wall at other times. Sliding doors also are a good solution. However this is managed, children do need open shelves so they can learn to take responsibility for getting out and putting away their own supplies.

These shelf areas need to be planned carefully. Items should not be stacked and crowded in ways the children cannot manage. Extra items should be stored in the teacher storage areas and only those for immediate use put on the children's shelves. And they should be changed from time to time. When children lose interest in one set of toys or puzzles or handwork materials, replace them with something new.

Individual "cubbies" are useful for children to store their own belongings—the papers they make, the purses or toys they bring, and so forth. If coats and overshoes are brought to the room, then open-front "lockers" are good. These facilities are not needed so much with small classes, but with large groups they help immensely to make life easier for the teachers. They also help give the children a feeling of belonging; many children need a space that is entirely theirs.

Large play equipment—both indoors and out—need not be expensive, and it should not consist wholly of the one-use traditional type of equipment. In recent years teachers began creatively planning their own play areas using cast-off barrels, boxes, old automobile parts, logs and other items. Then manufacturers caught the idea too, and they began designing multiple-use play equipment. So now you can have it either way—the expensive way, or the lower cost, homemade way. Children like something to climb, to hang from, to balance on, to crawl in; or something to roll, to pile up, or carry around.

Arranging the room takes creativity, too. Just as your home is planned with areas for different kinds of activities, for various group sizes, for privacy and togetherness, for noise and for quiet, so you need to think through carefully the traffic patterns and uses of the areas in your room. Are floor toys or games used where people walk over them? Are noisy activities placed next to quiet ones? Research shows that in a completely open space children tend to be noisier than if some areas are visually blocked off from others. Low partitions which block the children's view but do not completely block the teacher's view are good.

You need a large empty space for your group activities. You need an easily traveled path through the whole room. And you need all areas accessible to supervision. These three considerations are essential to any plan. Additional planning for learning centers or for nooks where children can get off alone will depend on the purposes you have and the kind of schedule and program you wish to offer.

Learning Centers

The materials and learning centers used in the room also should be dependent on the kind of program offered. To illustrate this important principle, we will consider the very familiar block center. In any standard preschool book the values given for block play will look something like this abbreviated list.

1.   Builds concepts of number, shape, space, weight, and so forth.
2.   Builds concepts of balance and support.
3.   Provides practice in visual and tactile discrimination.
4.   Provides movement and builds muscle coordination.
5.   Provides opportunity for problem solving.
6.   Provides opportunity for experimentation.
7.   Helps increase vocabulary—(square, long, high, and so forth).
8.   Provides escape from human inter-personal world to the world of materials.
9.   Provides opportunity to create own individual world.
10.   Provides opportunity to achieve and build self-concept.

Bible teachers sometimes try to use blocks for building the temple, or some other lesson-related activity, but this overlooks the fact that children's fascination for blocks comes with doing their own thing with them and not the teacher's thing. In one well-equipped classroom a man on the teaching team valiantly and enthusiastically worked at getting children to help him build up the temple walls. Some children did for a moment or two before moving on to something else. Some delighted in knocking the walls down, after which they left to explore other parts of the room. A fellow teacher with a stopwatch found that no child stayed with the temple job for more than two minutes. But meanwhile a boy laid a long road of blocks across the carpet. At the end of his road he began building a garage. He worked at his task twenty-five minutes and would have worked longer yet, but all the children were called at that time from their activities to the story circle.

Block play has many values, but Christian educators need to consider carefully how much they can add to a Sunday school or church program. Will the shelf space and floor space and time that they take be justified in terms of the needs and the goals of the particular church? Some people will decide yes and others will decide no.

Similarly, each church should decide concerning other kinds of learning centers—housekeeping or home centers, nature centers, book centers, music centers, art centers, and so forth. Some of these will have more value than others to a particular teaching program. Considerations of space and time also enter into the decisions. Teaching styles and basic philosophy affect the use of centers, too. Those who prefer to use as much time as possible for group learning experiences will have less time to use for individualized learning at the centers.

Teachers who want to use centers but have very limited space can, with ingenuity, plan one or two centers anyway. Learning centers need not be so formal as to require a blocked off area and a lot of equipment. A child sitting on the floor listening to a tape through earphones while the other children are seated around a table doing handwork can be said to be experiencing a music or story center. The earphones separate him from the rest of the class; they can proceed with their activity and he with his. A couple of children looking at picture books on the floor also are having the advantages of a learning center. There may be no room for rocking chairs, pillows and book display cases. The teacher may just set down the books when the children ask for them, and the books may have to be put away as soon as they are through, but for the time being it is their learning center. In this way teachers have provided many activities for the children even in their closet size rooms. One teacher allowed water play; two children at a time could play with boats in a plastic tub on the floor while the other children worked at the table.

Teachers need to use ingenuity to get the best use of the space they have, but at the same time a good many of them should also be appealing to the appropriate boards and committees for more space.

READING CHECK

1. Parents should not sneak away when the child is looking in another direction.   T   F
2. If a child acts silly or bullies others he probably needs a spanking.   T   F
3. Short, one-hour preschool sessions do not always need play time included.   T   F
4. A longer schedule needs to provide for active play, quiet play, rest, toileting, and nourishment.   T   F
5. Space requirements will vary according to the type of program offered.   T   F
6. Shelves should have doors and locks so the children do not get into things.   T   F
7. Learning centers are essential to a Sunday school program.   T   F

Answers: 1—T, 2—F, 3—T, 4—T, 5—T, 6—F, 7—F

8 Teacher in the Classroom

Raymond

Raymond entered his preschool classroom one Sunday and announced, "I'm four now. I can paint and color and everything. When I'm four I can do things."

The teacher could hardly believe her ears. Raymond was her child who came to tears almost every Sunday screaming "I can't, I can't" in frustration over his activities that never seemed to go as easily as he wanted.

"I'm going to paint," Raymond continued, as he walked to the shelf for paper. "I want to paint today. I'm four."

The usual procedure was for painting and other free handwork activities to come toward the end of the hour. The teacher fleetingly thought of asking Raymond to wait, but she stopped her words before they came out. She sensed that something important was happening and she had better not interfere. Other children began arriving. The teacher and Raymond shared with them the big event—Raymond was four. Some stood around watching what Raymond could do now that he was four. Others, seeing there was no gathering for story time, seized the opportunity to get out some toys, which usually were not allowed until later in the hour.

"Now, what have I done?" thought the teacher. "Our

routine has gone out the window and I may be in for bedlam here in a short time." But in a short time Raymond had painted several sheets of paper, everyone had duly admired them, and he was ready to put things away. "When you're four you remember where to put your paint shirt, your brush and everything." The teacher wasn't going to let that good opportunity pass. She also explained to the other children that they should put their things away too, and all should gather for story time.

The rest of the hour went more or less normally, except that everyone seemed a little more grown up on Raymond's big day. And even though this is a true story and not fiction, Raymond's new attitude continued. Sunday after Sunday the confident new Raymond came to enrich the class and remind the teacher that all her children were growing and developing.

Tricia

In another classroom shy little Tricia had come for the first time. Children were sitting at tables working puzzles. Tricia sat at a table and her big eyes and her mind tried to take in her surroundings. Tricia didn't have a puzzle; she didn't know anything about the puzzle cupboard where she could help herself, she was not aggressive enough to try to take one from another child, and the teacher was too busy to notice her. So she just sat, watching and thinking.

After a time Tricia saw the children and teacher together put the puzzles away in a cupboard. The teacher firmly closed the door and the puzzles all disappeared. Then the chairs were arranged in a partial circle, and Tricia was led to a seat where she sat very still. She didn't sing or say the Bible verse or do the fingerplays or interrupt the story. Her mind may have been active with a hundred things but none could know about that; they could only see how still she sat.

After a very long time Tricia saw the teacher get up and do something in a black box. Then music started and all the children began marching around the room. Tricia was led to the line and she marched too. The music stopped and she looked for her chair. It was gone. The whole circle was gone. Children began sitting around the tables where the chairs were, so Tricia found an empty chair and sat down too.

The teacher was busy at the big table walking around it, giving something to the children, and talking to them. Two girls sat at Tricia's small table, quiet, waiting. Tricia looked at her empty table and at the cupboard door, then looked at her table again. She left her seat, went to the cupboard, got a puzzle and took it back to her table. She was just getting some pieces spread out ready for working the puzzle when the teacher came over.

"No," snapped the teacher, grabbing up everything. "This is not the time for playing. We're supposed to work our sheets now."

Teaching Styles

Teachers have differing views of their roles. A good many of them probably are influenced by what "Teacher" was to them back in their own school days. They are not likely to remember well a teacher from the year they were 3, but they remember other teachers—perhaps some who knew all the answers and told you when you were wrong, or who assigned work to do and told you whether you did it well enough. Often in these memories the teacher's job was to control, and the child's was to conform.

Tricia's teacher, as depicted above, may appear to be insensitive to children's needs and harshly authoritarian. But actually she is a hard-working, dedicated teacher busy with a large class, who tries to keep things under control by teaching the children a regular routine. Her action in this case was meant to teach Tricia the routine that after marching time comes the time to work on take-home sheets. As she was intent on keeping the routine working, she missed seeing what remarkable learning Tricia had accomplished on her first day. Tricia learned that at the tables children can work puzzles. She also learned where the puzzles were stored, and in her quiet, self-sufficient way she was acting upon her learning.

This one rebuff is not likely to stop Tricia from learning. She can extend her learning in this case, adjusting it to see that *sometimes* at the tables she can work puzzles. She also can learn a little more about putting up with busy and impatient teachers, and that learning may be more useful than the other. A continuous diet of such rebuffs to learning and self-sufficiency can have the effect of crushing a spirit. Tricia could learn not to think or act for herself, but just to be a docile classroom body, letting the teacher do all the thinking and tell her what to do.

Raymond's teacher, too, tried to keep a certain routine about her teaching hour, and she had twangs of guilt feelings when she allowed the children to disrupt the routine. But the happy rewards of that incident are likely to lessen her guilt the next time. Teachers learn, as well as the children.

Keeping a classroom routine is not the only technique that gives teachers a sense of control and a feeling that they are actually "teaching." Another area for control is the children's work. Some teachers hover over the children seeing that they get this sticker and that sticker in the "right" place, seeing that they use the "right" color, admonishing them to stay within the lines, and on and on. What is teaching if it's not telling children how to do it better and do it right?

A strange reversal of this kind of teaching has come into vogue in recent years. Teachers have been told that children should not be criticized and crushed in their early efforts, but what they need is praise and encouragement. So teachers act like the one who sat at a round table with ten children stringing macaroni. Her running speech hardly stopped. "That's great, Roger. You're doing a fantastic job, Julia. What nice work, Gretchen! Oh, I like yours. Fantastic! Super! Wonderful!" This teacher hardly looked at what was going on. She was busy sorting colored macaroni, but carrying out her teaching role as she perceived it.

Some teachers even don a certain voice which is not their normal speaking voice at all. It is a voice which says, "Now, my little children, I am talking to you." Symptoms such as this may be indications of people playing the role of teacher as opposed to actually being teacher.

Finding Your Style

Being teacher of little children is difficult, and it is no wonder people try out so many styles of teaching as they search for their own comfortable way. If God is calling you into this work, it is helpful to remember that He calls *you*. You will not need to speak with a different voice and become a different person in the classroom.

You may be Mrs. Orderlove who feels comfortable with your children seated in a straight row of chairs as you lead them through a precise routine of songs, prayer and stories. Then you move them to a round table and lead them through almost as precise a routine of handwork. Rest time, refreshment time, and even play time pass just as predictably, and hardly a child is out of place.

Or you may be Mrs. Lessayfare who can sit on the floor reading a story to just one child, while two children across the room are painting, some more are seated at a table doing various things, and still more are wandering around looking for something to do.

Who can say just what the teacher should be? Researchers cannot. Attempts have been made to measure how much the teacher talks, how much she listens to pupils, how many encouraging remarks she makes, and numerous other aspects of classroom behavior. But these researches have not brought to us a description of the ideal teacher. Attempts have been made to compare various teaching methods, and though methods pass in and out of vogue, researchers cannot prescribe for us the best method to use.

Some people like to speak of the "science of education" and others object that education is not a science. But whatever it is, it has not yet been able to identify the vital inner core of a good teacher and tell what makes him or her different from ineffective, poor teachers. There is speculation now that much of the effectiveness lies in the interpersonal relationships between teacher and pupils. If this is so, it is what our Christian view has told us all along. Also if this is so, it means you will need genuine respect for your children as little persons. No set of techniques practiced in roleplay fashion will do the job by itself.

A pastor involved in helping Christians behind the Iron Curtain writes that it is easy to tell real Christians from imposters by the way the Christians can look closely into each other's eyes. When the Communists caught on to this they began training their people to look closely into the Christians' eyes. But they were still detected because they looked too closely. If they should ever master this one technique there will be others to give them away. A counterfeit Christian brother cannot be made like the real thing.

So it is with the teacher. Be the real thing. Be you. Then you will not have to worry so much about which is the right style of operating in the classroom.

You Can't Do It All

Many times you will find yourself in situations where you have to react according to your own intuition. No book has told you what to do. In fact, the books may have given you an unrealistic impression of the preschool classroom.

Some Sunday Donald may come in with his hyperactive cousin Britt. If Britt has visited before, you steel yourself for a difficult session. Britt is on the move all the time and he takes Donald with him. You no sooner gather everyone in a story circle then Britt and Donald are off crawling under the table. You coax and entice and scold but nothing works. You forcibly bring them back and start your story. Britt interrupts, walks around, talks cheerfully about his dog. You ignore what you can, handle what you can and soon Britt and Donald are back under the table. "Let them stay," you decide. "It's better without them." You turn a bit so the children's backs are toward the table and you work to hold the attention of the rest of the children. But it gets noisier and noisier back there and more boys are slipping off to join the table play.

Or maybe a child begins a loud, screaming cry. You pick her up and begin walking around, talking comfortingly to her. She will quiet down soon, you think. But she doesn't. She screams on and on.

Or a little girl wets a big puddle on the floor. You try to locate a mop or rags. You wonder what to do about the child's clothes. There are no diapers; this class is supposed to be too old for that.

Or the barometer is falling and no child acts as he normally does. They don't know what's wrong and neither do you as you struggle against the unseen power in the air.

A good many problems could be handled if there were an extra teacher, and many would be minimized if there were plenty of space. Church planners need to realize these essentials. Preschool classrooms need more space per pupil than any other age.

What actually happens in many churches is that the preschool class gets tucked away in one of the smallest rooms there is. If you are in this kind of situation and you can figure out any solution, you should suggest it to the appropriate person or committee. And be prepared to keep after them. Be the squeaking wheel for a while, because that is the one which will get oiled.

But if you see no immediate solution, only a long-range one such as a new building, you may as well settle down to figuring out how to make the best of what you have. In a small space and a large class with only one teacher, you get along better with a more highly structured program. Plan a full session of activities. Have all supplies laid out and ready. Remove noisy toys and the ones which wheel around and need space. Keep only the kind that children sit and play with quietly. Don't use the toys every week. Save them for the days when a Britt or a crying little girl makes it impossible for you to go on with your plans.

Your children may be housebroken but they are not yet classroom broken. The Sundays when everything seems to fail are part of the process of breaking these children in to the classroom. No one should promise you a rose garden when you take this job, but there will be roses along the way.

Delores

For a couple of Sundays Delores sat where the teacher set her. But that was all she did. She never opened her mouth to speak or sing. She never picked up a crayon to scribble on her paper. The teacher began to wonder if she was retarded. Did she know how to talk at all?

One Sunday Delores discovered the toys. Someone opened the cupboard and she found a toy and sat beside the cupboard happily holding it. After that Delores' place was by the toy cupboard. If the teacher tried to move her or to put the toy away, she objected with a closed-lip crying, "Mm-mm." So Sunday after Sunday Delores sat in her chosen place. She was quiet and bothered no one.

Other children whined, "Why can't I play with toys? Delores is."

"You're bigger. You know how to come to story time. Let's show Delores how we read our stories."

When they sang "Jesus loves Tommy and Angela" and all the other children they included Delores too. When each child told how he obeys at home and the teacher wrote it in a book, she made a page for Delores too. "What does your mother ask you to do, Delores?" No answer. "I know. Mother says to put your pajamas on, so Delores runs and puts her pajamas on. Here is smiling Delores and she obeys her mother."

On the following Sundays the book remembered that Delores puts her pajamas on. That was always there with the other children's stories. The Bible stories were repeated, too, and the songs and action rhymes.

One day there was a big snowstorm and hardly anyone came to church. Instead of fourteen children, there were three in the preschool class and what a surprise the teacher had! Delores chattered like any normal child. She knew all the Bible stories and could fill in the missing word when the teacher waited for the children to help. She knew the songs and rhymes. She colored her paper. During her quiet days she had been learning a lot, but she just hadn't been able to show it until the day when there were only three children in class.

Much of your teaching with preschoolers will be like this. You cannot test and see what the results are. You observe, but only a small portion of the results are showing. You patiently teach and teach week after week and the greatest part of your work remains hidden. It is in the seedling tree—and you cannot see the giant that lies inside.

READING CHECK

1. Research evidence does not support one particular style of teaching over another.   T   F
2. When things go wrong it must be because the teacher has not planned carefully enough.   T   F
3. By tests and observations a teacher should be able to determine the results of teaching.   T   F
4. Many results of teaching are not immediately apparent in little children.   T   F

Appendix

In this section are study helps for each chapter, which can be used when this book is studied in classrooms or in church training groups.

CHAPTER 1: WHAT ARE THE CHILDREN LIKE?

Questions *(for discussion or for essay topics)*
1. Have you ever learned something by accident? Do you think everything you learn is for the purpose of meeting your needs?
2. Do you see needs as the "cause" of learning, or do you see learning as a cause or means of growing to more mature emotional levels on the "needs pyramid"? Do you think this is a chicken and egg question?
3. The "needs" theory teaches that learning is for need reduction. Piagetian theory teaches that learning takes place because the developing individual reaches out to learn. Which theory do you like better? Why? How does each theory fit with a Biblical view?
4. What spiritual growth, if any, do you think happens in a child too young to understand his need for salvation?
5. What do you think is the church's responsibility in the spiritual nurture of young children?

Study Projects
1. Read more about the young child's thought in a book by Piaget or about Piagetian theory. Report to your study

group what you learn.

    2.   Find something about the young child's thinking written by Jerome Bruner. Report to your study group what you learn.

Observations

    1.   Observe a child in a situation where he has a choice of activity free from adult direction and free from other children's distractions. List one or more of his activities and the length of time he stays at each. Compare your observations with those of others in your study group.

    2.   Observe a preschool class. Watch not only the formal teaching, but any small, incidental happenings. Try to find incidents that can affect a child's growth, one in each of these three areas: (1) spiritual, (2) cognitive, and (3) social-emotional. Describe each.

Mini-Teaching Experiences

    1.   Plan a task resembling the Piaget mountain experiment and try it out with one or two four-year-olds. (You need children old enough to be capable of drawing what they see.)

    2.   With one child of preschool age read books or play with his toys or any activity he will like. Share your experience with others in your group, telling what you learned about words the child uses, his attention span, his curiosity and other characteristics.

CHAPTER 2: WHAT CAN THE CHILDREN LEARN?

Questions

    1.   Do you think a child's concrete idea of God is a distorted idea? Are his later learnings corrections or additions to and development of his earlier learning?

2.   Given the child's concrete view of the person of God, what differences will there be in the way a liberal teaches and the way a conservative or fundamentalist teaches about God?

3.   With young children would you use the term God-Man, or God's Son, or some other? Why?

4.   Use the story of Noah and the flood or any other your group chooses and make lists of ideas preschool children can and cannot learn from it. Try to agree on one or two major ideas to emphasize if you were to use this story in teaching.

5.   What do you think preschool children can learn about angels? About sin?

Study Projects

1.   Find another writer's list or discussion of what Bible ideas children can learn, and compare that with what is given in this chapter. Identify any differences, tell what you think about those cases, and why you think as you do.

2.   Use a tape recorder and record three-minute segments of time in which you play and talk with a two-year-old and a four-year-old. Try to get each child to talk as much as you can. List the total number of words spoken by each child and the number of different words spoken by each. Comment on what you learn from these lists.

Classroom Observation

Choose one child to watch during the period of your observation. Make notes about his use of words. Here are some things to look for. How much does he participate in songs and rhymes? Does he repeat words the teacher wants everyone to say? Does he use words to get what he wants from the teacher and others, or does he use other means—either quiet, self-sufficient means or aggressive means? How many times does he talk *to* someone, and how many times does he simply talk? Do you observe any times when he seems to be saying words just for the sake of saying them? List the Bible or lesson-related words you hear him say. Does he

TEACHING PRESCHOOLERS

interrupt the lesson with unrelated talk? What is this talk about?

Mini-Teaching Experiences
1. Join a preschool snack time. Take a tape recorder if you can, or at least jot down notes immediately afterward. Share your experience with others in your study group.
2. Choose a picture and lead a preschool class in conversation about it. Share your experience with your study group.

CHAPTER 3: WHAT HANDWORK CAN CHILDREN DO?

Questions
1. Do you remember using coloring books? What do you think they did for you?
2. How important do you think handwork is to your church's goals? About how much time should be devoted to it each week?
3. What do you think are the most important values of handwork?
4. Can you think of some kinds of children who may gain more from handwork at church than others? What kinds?
5. What qualities and skills does a teacher need to direct handwork time with young children?

Study Projects
1. Interview an art teacher about teaching children to color within lines. Share the views you hear with your study group.
2. Gather several children's drawings of people and try to arrange them in order from simplest to most advanced. You may wish to include pictures from kindergarten and primary departments in this study.

148

Observations

1.   Watch some children as they color on blank paper and listen to their comments as they work. Try to find a child in each of these stages: (1) scribble stage, (2) recognition stage, (3) representational stage.

2.   Watch some children doing any kind of handwork. Write out one or two incidents you observe in which some kind of growth besides art skill may be happening.

Mini-Teaching Experiences

1.   Prepare clay and arrange to sit with one tableful of children and have a "clay session" with them. If interest lags, be ready to inject a new idea. See if you can keep the session going well for at least ten minutes.

2.   If you prefer some other medium besides clay, plan similarly for painting, pasting or something else.

CHAPTER 4: WHAT ABOUT MUSIC AND RHYMES?

Questions

1.   What do you see in some action rhymes that makes it possible for children to learn them?

2.   What features about some action rhymes make them too difficult to learn?

3.   Why do you think many teachers lack confidence for teaching music? Are these reasons things that can be overcome? How?

4.   If you felt your class of children was not enjoying music, what are some things you could do about it?

Study Projects

1.   Prepare several of your favorite action rhymes on cards—one rhyme per card. Make a second set of cards with

words for some of the songs you would like to use when you teach.

2.   Make a set of rhythm instruments, such as rhythm sticks or pill bottle shakers.

3.   Choose one or two lesson topics and make up a song to go with each one. Use a familiar nursery rhyme tune such as "Farmer in the Dell," or make your own tune if you wish.

Observation

Observe a preschool music time. Choose one child to watch. Write a report of your observation and comment on things such as these. How much does the child participate? In what ways does he participate—singing, lips moving, doing motions? Does he participate equally on all songs? Does he sing along with the teacher, or is he usually a phrase or so behind? When he is not overtly participating, does he seem to be watching and listening? What feature(s) of the song time seem to attract him most? How would you describe this child's developmental level in singing?

Mini-Teaching Experience

Prepare and present a five-minute session of songs and rhymes. To make a good session don't just do lots of songs one after the other, but plan ways to use each song or rhyme several times with variety to give children time to digest it before moving on to something new. For instance, on one song use a hand or finger puppet and give children turns wearing it. Use a song with children's names and sing about all the children in the group. Use motions, or use rhythm instruments. Or take turns rocking a doll as you sing a lullaby. Plan a varied session and learn it well so you can give your attention to the children and not to your song cards and supplies.

CHAPTER 5: HOW DO YOU HANDLE STORIES?

Questions

1.　How important do you think Bible stories are to your church's goals? How much time should be devoted to stories each week?

2.　What problems do you see in each of these opening story sentences?

> A week before Christmas Jodi got a present.
>
> Once a long time ago the world was full of people who forgot about God.
>
> There was once a little girl who had been taken far away from her own people and her own land.

3.　Can you remember watching flannelgraph when you were a child? What are some of your memories about it?

Study Project

Read a Bible story from any preschool story paper or teacher's manual. Analyze it in terms of: (1) causal relationships, (2) family relationships, (3) other relationships, (4) space concepts, (5) time concepts. If you find any problems, try to rewrite the story to eliminate the problems.

Observation

Observe a story time either at church or at a public library, or both. Choose one child to watch. Write a report of your observation of the child and comment on these things. What about his posture and movements? Does he wiggle legs, change position, turn head, watch the teacher, etc? How much of the time does he watch intently? How much of the time is he doing other things? Do his lips sometimes move as he listens? Does he participate in audible ways? Does he interrupt with seemingly irrelevant comments? Does he participate in movement activities? What things seem to distract him? What things about the planned story time catch his attention?

Mini-Teaching Experience

Plan and present a story time that will last at least ten minutes. You may use several picture books and one or more flannelgraph stories. Have some action rhymes or play-the-story ideas ready to intersperse action between stories as needed to hold attention. You may also use a song or two. Try to relate some of the songs or rhymes you use to a story.

CHAPTER 6: WHAT ABOUT GAMES AND MOVEMENT?

Questions

1.   Do you see games as belonging primarily to the teaching or to the recreational aspect of a preschool session? Why?

2.   If you met a teacher who feels that games have no part in a Bible teaching program, how could you justify games to this person?

3.   Why are each of these not appropriate in young children's games? (1) Competition, (2) cooperation, (3) scoring.

Study Projects

1.   Choose one or two lesson topics and design a pretend game for each. Design also a singing game or card game for each of the same lessons. (Many published lessons now include games, so you will not often have to do this in your lesson preparation, but the experience of designing games will make you a better evaluator of games and lesson materials.)

2.   Examine preschool (or nursery) lessons from two or more publishers. Evaluate them on their use of games.

3.   Choose a game you like, and write a paragraph or two telling how you can justify it from an educational standpoint. Tell both how it fits the child's developmental

level and what he can gain from it cognitively, socio-emotionally, and physically.

Mini-Teaching and Observation

Work with a partner on this. Each of you prepare a game of a different type. For instance, one of you can prepare a card game and the other, a singing game. Arrange to have a few moments time with a group of preschool children. While one leads a game the other observes, then exchange places for the second game.

Observation tasks. How many different kinds or levels of participation can you find and describe? Do some children just sit, others participate in some parts, and others participate fully? What seems to help most to get children to think or act purposefully? What distracts some children?

Evaluation. Do your observation notes suggest to you any way the games might be modified to obtain fuller participation or higher interest. How? Do they suggest any better way for the teacher to get things started quickly, or keep the interest high? How?

CHAPTER 7: PROCEDURES, EQUIPMENT, ENVIRONMENT

Questions

Would you include these centers in your preschool room at church? Tell why or why not for each one.

Block center	Nature center
Art center	Book center
Housekeeping center	Music center
Puzzle and table games center	Dress-up center
	Sand play center

Study Projects

1.   Inspect the preschool room or rooms in your church, with a team if possible, and plan how they might be improved. Write a list of things that might be done and try to justify each suggested change. Why is it needed? How will it be better than now?

2.   Draw what you consider an ideal room plan, and list the equipment needed for it.

Observation

Observe a class while the children are arriving. Watch what each child does in the first minute or so. Does he seem eager or afraid? How does he greet the teacher? Does he move immediately to an activity? Does he watch others? Write notes about as many of the children as you can. Share your observations with others in your study group.

Mini-Teaching Experience

Help a preschool teacher with her class at arrival time and/or at goodbye time. Greet children and parents, help with coats and other necessities. Try to make both times happy and relaxed. Help children feel welcome but not pressured to begin an activity immediately. If the children do not know you, be careful about forcing your attentions on them more than they are ready to accept. Share with your study group some things you learn from this experience. Do you see any way to make things go better if you do it again?

CHAPTER 8: TEACHER IN THE CLASSROOM

Questions

1.   What do you think are some good ways for a teacher to keep control in the classroom?

2.   Do you think children do better under a laissez-faire style of teaching or under a highly structured one? Why?

3.   Do you think any particular style of teaching fits Christian education goals better than others? Which one? Why?

Study Project

Describe one of the most difficult problems you encountered while studying this course. It can have to do with facilities, a child (use a fictional name), lessons, or any other aspect. Work with a small group to plan how to approach a solution to your problem and to the other problems the group presents.

Classroom Observations

1.   Describe a teacher-directed activity. Tell how the teacher leads it and how the children respond and learn from it.

2.   Describe something a child does on his own—perhaps an incident similar to Tricia getting the puzzle. Tell what motive or thinking you would guess is behind the action.

Maxi-Teaching Experience

With a partner or team from your study group, plan a full hour session for Sunday school or another time. You can use a published lesson as the basis for your plan. Prepare everything, and teach the lesson. Share something from this experience with your study group.

Index

Other books by this author:

Teaching Kindergartners
Teaching Primaries
Teaching Juniors
Songs for Young Children
Teacher's Handbook of Instant Activities
A Biblical Psychology of Learning

Card Packets:

Bible Learning Games
Bible Rhymes to Say and Do

ACCENT TEACHER TRAINING SERIES